SMART GOVERNMENT

A PARLIAMENT STREET GUIDE TO BETTER
AND MORE EFFICIENT GOVERNMENT

Edited by

Patrick J. Sullivan
and
Nabil H. Najjar

Smart Government: A Parliament Street Guide to Better and More Effective Government

© Parliament Street 2015. All rights reserved.

Designed and printed in the UK by

Delta Strategies Ltd
Mount Pleasant
Salisbury
England
www.DeltaStrategies.co.uk

No part of this publication may be reproduced, stored in a retrieval system, or transmitted in any form or by any means without the prior permission in writing of the publisher, nor be otherwise circulated in any form of binding or cover other than that in which it is published and without a similar condition being imposed on the subsequent purchaser.

Parliament Street holds no corporate view, and all opinions expressed within are solely those of their respective authors, and do not necessarily reflect the opinions of Parliament Street or its Executive Board.

ISBN: 978-0-9932230-0-6

CONTENTS

Foreword 5
The Rt. Hon. Liam Fox M.P.

How Do We Build Generations of Game Changers? 7
Michael Mercieca

Local Homes for Local People 19
Cllr. Tom Hunt

Time for a Dose of Euro-Realism 35
Shaun Bailey and Nabil Najjar

Islamic Extremism: the Greatest Threat to Britain's Future 47
Clare George-Hilley

New Energy, New Jobs 53
Aisha Vance and Dr. James P. Verdon

Giving Public Services a Tech Injection 64
Steven George-Hilley

Immigration: Public Opinion & Policy 69
Mo Metcalf-Fisher and James Downes

A Very British Constitution ..86

Matthew Gass

Conservatives Trust Schools ... 102

Steven Mastin

Recommendations for 'Phase II' of the UK's Economic Recovery ... 116

Luke Springthorpe

Any Man Politics ... 134

Maeve Clare Ambrosino

Afterword ... 142

Patrick Sullivan

FOREWORD

There are a number of things that have hugely impressed me about this, the first Parliament Street publication. The first is the breadth of thinking, covering a wide range of areas, from energy policy to immigration and from Islamic fundamentalism to the role of technology in government. In an election that already looks like having a depressingly narrow policy base, this is both welcome and refreshing. The second is the very personal nature of the writing and the passion contained within it, drawing on the wide background of contributors from business, politics, academia and, importantly, none of the above.

The combination of these gives the feel of an agenda coming up from the grassroots rather than pontifications from on high. While the contributions do not lack ideological fervour, they nonetheless produce practical steps to deal with many of the problems considered. I cannot say that I completely agreed with some of the contributions but that is rather the point, to challenge the reader and stimulate what is often lacking in our contemporary politics – a real debate about the most important, not the most convenient issues.

Parliament Street has become an important part of the wider Conservative family and this publication emphasises one of its most important aspects – that the British Conservative movement has traditionally been a wide coalition of interests. The Conservative party has been electorally stronger when it represents a wider, rather than a narrower, spectrum of views and "Smart Government" is a timely reminder of this.

The Rt. Hon. Liam Fox M.P.

Member of Parliament for Woodspring and former Secretary of State for Defence

HOW DO WE BUILD GENERATIONS OF GAME CHANGERS?

Michael Mercieca, Chief Executive of Young Enterprise, discusses how skills and financial education can help young people prepare for the challenges of work and life

INTRODUCTION

"Building Generations of Game Changers" focuses on the future facing the UK's young people. As the UK climbs out of the recession and into recovery, the challenge for young people leaving education is getting that first crucial step on the career ladder.

The "Game" is the difficult situation young people face, and those "Game Changers" we need to create are the next and future generations that will be creative, resilient, and able to apply their academic and employment skills to starting a business or to their chosen profession. In a recent landmark report, fund managers Octopus Investments found that high-growth small businesses (HGSBs) account for just 1% of businesses but generated 68% of new jobs in the UK between 2012 and 2013. These 30,000 HGSBs are highly profitable and grow fast, generating significant economic growth. These are the Game Changers that we need more of.

The problem to be tackled, which will be explored in depth here, is four-pronged: the gap between the skills young people finish education with and the skills required by employers, high youth unemployment, a rapidly changing global economy and a need for financial capability.

Thankfully, youth unemployment is falling slowly, but it is still nearly triple the headline rate for 16-64 year olds. With increases in the retirement age, it may take years for the rates to equalise, if they ever do. All the more reason for changing the way we educate young people.

As the UK's leading enterprise and financial education charity, Young Enterprise calls for a joined up, long-term skills strategy that works for young people, teachers, tutors and employers.

Young Enterprise has extensive experience in delivering 'skills education' that works. Following the merger of pfeg, (Personal Financial Education Group) into Young Enterprise in September 2014, we are a one-stop-shop of teaching and resources for students and teachers. We know that what we do, and what we're calling for, works.

THE CHALLENGES FACED BY YOUNG PEOPLE

Youth unemployment is at 16.6% for the period of August to October 2014. This continues the recent downward trend, but the rate remains higher than the pre-downturn rate of 13.8% for December 2007 to February 2008, and higher than the 6.5% headline rate for 16-64 year olds.

This continued fall is encouraging, and may reflect a slow return to pre-economic crash levels. However, the fall cannot merely be attributed to a rise in the number of jobs. Other factors play a part and must be taken into account; a rise in part time work and a rise in zero-contract hours are two such factors.

Everyone who has finished education and gone into work knows the feeling of entering the great unknown of employment. Self-employment, whilst just as unknown, is more flexible as the rules are not fixed. The skills required however, are broadly the same.

The world is rapidly changing, and what may have worked ten or twenty years ago is growing consistently less relevant to the global employment market. Competition is heating up as markets open up; young people are no longer competing with their peers from their degree class or college tutorials. Entry-level roles are more demanding as employers need to see more from their newest recruits. These new challenges must be taken into consideration when writing education policy that works for everyone.

Research carried out by Opinium with Young Enterprise found that 70% of employers in the UK say it is difficult to find entry level recruits with the right skills for the role. These skills aren't specific to particular roles; communication, people skills, self-management, teamwork and a positive attitude – skills we expect to develop during school, college and university.[1]

Moreover, 43% of UK employers say the education system is not equipping young people with the right skills for them to enter the workforce.[2]

This is the 'skills crisis' that is gaining more attention in education discussions, in Parliament and in the media.

The former Education Secretary, Michael Gove, believed a more rigorous academic approach was the answer to improving schools' examination results. Sound academic results are core to young people's success and provide a level against which to measure.

---

[1] Young Enterprise and Citi Foundation Opinium research of 418 senior managers in the UK, Spain, France and Germany 2014
[2] Ibid

However, measuring against one value or set of values is too narrow Sfor today's young people. Academic results are of course important, but shouldn't be taken as the be all and end all for future success.

Ofsted's latest annual report for 2013/14 found that secondary schools are struggling to sustain the progress of recent years. The report also noted that "too many institutions are still not equipping learners with the knowledge and skills that employers seek."[3]

The gap between the knowledge and skills with which young people leave the education system and those required by employers should be a Key Performance Indicator (KPI) of the education system.

This skills gap affects everyone finishing education, whether that is after A Levels or after a degree. Moreover, 88% of British businesses recognise that a workforce with the right skills is critical to the growth of their organisation, with another 73% believing a skills crisis will hit the UK within the next three years.[4]

There is also a fundamental need for financial capability, as young people grow up in an increasingly complex world that requires them to make difficult financial decisions. They need to make informed choices about money at an early age, and they bear more financial risk in adulthood due to increased life expectancy, a decrease in welfare benefits and uncertain economic and job prospects.

---

[3] 'Annual Report', Her Majesty's Chief Inspector of Education, Children's Services and Skills 2013/14
[4] 'Upskilling the Workforce of the Future ', The Prince's Trust, 2014

Lastly, the changing economy means that young people are more likely to have multiple careers with various employers, ranging from global multinationals to small and micro-employers.[5]

A complex problem requires a multi-faceted solution that works for everyone.

MULTI-FACETED SOLUTIONS

This solution lies in a joined up education policy that directly addresses the skills gap, giving teachers and students the support they need to tackle it.

The Education Secretary Nicky Morgan unveiled in December 2014 ambitious plans that will see £5m of funding allocated to support new, innovative projects that build character, resilience and grit.

In her announcement, Morgan noted that: "It is clear that many schools and colleges need additional support if we are to ensure every young person – regardless of background or location – receives the life-changing advice and inspiration that they need to fulfil their potential and succeed in life."[6]

Morgan's main proposal of a government-funded company, run by Capgemini UK Chairman Christine Hodgson, that will support much greater engagement between employers, schools and colleges, should ensure young people have better access to the guidance they need to finish education ready for work, and is a positive step towards ensuring young people have access to the skills education they need.

---

[5] 'Enterprise for All', Lord Young, June 2014
[6] Statement by the Right Honourable Nicky Morgan in the House of Commons on preparing young people for the world of work, Dec 2014

We are looking forward to working with this new company as it will expand on the work Young Enterprise already does. We work with 6,000 business volunteers from 3,500 companies, putting them in the classroom so that students can learn first-hand from their future colleagues about the world of work.

Morgan's announcement also included the development of an Enterprise Passport, proposed originally in Lord Young's Enterprise for All report, after it was proposed by Young Enterprise as part of our input to the report. This Passport would measure students' skills development and encourage young people to participate in extra-curricular activities which will boost their chances when applying for jobs.

Employers currently aren't able to measure key skills development when interviewing for entry-level roles, and instead must go on a candidate's performance during interview and their CV. The Passport would provide students with a physical record of their development, to sit alongside their academic achievements.

The timing of the announcement was key as it came on the same day as Ofsted's report, in which Sir Michael Wilshaw noted his concerns at the lack of skills education, with too many young people leaving schools and colleges without the skills and attitudes employers are looking for. Sir Michael noted that: "Despite there being around one million young people aged 16-24 not in work, education or training[7], employers report that almost three in every 10 vacancies are hard to fill."[8]

---

[7] 'Going in the right direction? Careers guidance in schools from September 2012 (10114)', Ofsted, Sep 2013
[8] 'Annual Report', Her Majesty's Chief Inspector of Education, Children's Services and Skills 2013/14

HOW DO WE BUILD GENERATIONS OF GAME CHANGERS

It is imperative to work with education providers to make good quality skills education available to young people, supporting teachers and tutors with the resources and training needed. It requires a joined-up approach between those who measure education standards and those who deliver education.

Young Enterprise is already one of the UK's leading providers of skills education, and following the merger of pfeg into Young Enterprise (YE), is the leading enterprise and financial education charity. We are well-placed to work closely with more schools, colleges, universities and businesses to ensure young people are prepared for work and for life.

In 2014/2015 we planned to work with over 290,000 young people in 818 primary schools, 168 FE colleges, 2,410 secondary schools ad 36 HE institutions.

It is through enterprise and financial education that we believe young people develop the key skills that employers are calling for. Enterprise education is the application of creative ideas to practical solutions, aiming to raise awareness of the mind-set and skills required to respond to opportunities, needs and challenges.

Financial education is a planned programme of study that equips young people with the knowledge, skills and confidence to manage their money well. Financial education improves understanding of attitudes to risk and the behaviours and emotions involved in financial decisions.

Pre-merger, Young Enterprise had been running since 1963, having been founded by investment banker Sir Walter Salomon in Chatham, Kent. Based on the USA's Junior Achievement programme, Salomon's vision was to foster work readiness, entrepreneurship and financial literacy skills through 'learning by doing'. Access for all is key to Young Enterprise's vision, and remains so today. Young Enterprise has worked with over four million young people across the UK. We work with over 250,000 young people delivering more than 2.3million enterprise teaching hours every year.

We know from our research that enterprise education works. 92% of Young Enterprise students increase at least one employability competency, with the biggest development being problem-solving.[9] Moreover, the Education and Employers Taskforce has found that young people who undertook four or more activities "involving employers or local business people providing things like mentoring, enterprise competitions, careers advice and CV or interview practice" were five times less likely to be not in employment, education or training (NEET) than those who had no such engagement while at school."[10] We know that enterprise education works.

pfeg has been a trusted provider of free advice, support and resources for anyone teaching children and young people how to manage money well since 2000. It has trained more than 20,000 teachers and provided over 280,000 resources to help teach financial education.

It offers a variety of programmes and services, and in 2011 was instrumental in establishing and providing the secretariat for the All Party Parliamentary Group (APPG) on Financial Education for Young People. The APPG's eight-month enquiry concluded that financial education should be taught as a compulsory part of the Secondary National Curriculum for England, which came into force in September 2014.

---

[9] Young Enterprise and Citi Foundation Opinium Research of 418 senior managers in the UK, Spain, France and Germany, 2014
[10] Young Enterprise Company Programme 2013-2014 Impact Report.

pfeg also partners with a range of businesses including Santander and Experian to transform schools into pfeg Centres of Excellence, which develops them into beacons of good practice for financial education.

Post-merger, pfeg's work remains focused on supporting education providers and others involved in teaching children and young people about money. Operating under the umbrella of Young Enterprise, its expertise in financial education coupled with YE's in enterprise education creates a strong force for skills education in the UK. We are a one stop shop of programmes, training and resources for young people and for teachers and tutors.

Our expertise in the education arena is strong, as evidenced by our 2015 Manifesto: Building Generations of Game Changers, where we look at the problem of the skills gap and crisis and set out our solution.

Fundamentally, our solution is a long term, sustainable skills strategy founded on enterprise and financial education. This must work for teachers, college tutors, youth workers, employers and young people.

A joined-up strategy is key to our approach, as we seek cross-party support to ensure it is long-term, sustainable and relevant.

As part of our 'Access for All' vision, this strategy must be embedded in all schools, colleges and universities across the UK and be owned by key government departments with equal accountability.

OUR STRATEGY

Our strategy includes seven clear points that we believe must be taken on board by all political parties if we are to address this crisis:

SMART GOVERNMENT: A PARLIAMENT STREET GUIDE

1) Tackle the skills gap identified by employers
2) Agree a long-term, sustainable skills strategy
3) Launch an Enterprise Skills Passport
4) Make financial education statutory in primary schools
5) Make Personal Social Health Economic education statutory
6) Ensure that Teacher Training programmes and Initial Teacher Training incorporate the five skills listed below
7) Work with Ofsted to build in reporting on enterprise education and financial education to their inspections.

The five key skills we are calling for are problem-solving, resilience, creativity, communication and teamwork. These take from the top five skills British employers believe young people should have when entering the workforce, and those they believe young people lack the most when applying for jobs.

We know that our programmes enable young people to develop these skills. Evaluation of our flagship Company Programme found that 90% of teachers agreed the Programme raised awareness of capabilities in their students, and 92% of the young people surveyed found they had improved in at least one employability competency, with communication, problem-solving and resilience seeing the greatest average point increase.[11]

pfeg's annual 'My Money Week' has since 2009 helped 4.3m young people understand money. Its Centres of Excellence programme currently has 76 registered Centres and has awarded Excellence status to 24 of those schools since 2013.

---

[11] Young Enterprise Company Programme 2013-2014 Impact Report.

HOW DO WE BUILD GENERATIONS OF GAME CHANGERS

Of our seven asks above, it is calling for financial education in primary schools that may seem controversial. After all, why do eight-year-olds need to understand money?

Young people today face more financial decisions than their parents ever did, and at an earlier age. Research carried out by pfeg found that 64% of children get their bank or building society account before they start secondary school, and nearly three-quarters of 15-year-olds with a bank account have a debit card.

pfeg's research also found that 94% of teachers[12] and 96% of young people[13] agree that financial education should be taught in schools. However fewer than a third of primary schools currently offer it.

Young Enterprise's newest programme for primary schools; the Fiver Challenge, launched with the support of Lord Young and BIS, and supported by Virgin Money, introduces children to business in a fun and creative environment. Pledged £5 and given a month to set up mini-businesses to make a profit, the Challenge saw 31,525 pupils from 447 schools register to take part in June 2014. Post-Challenge evaluation reported that 76% of supervisors found their pupils developed at least one employability skill during the month.

Our vision of 'Access for All' extends to our programmes offer. Together with pfeg we work with young people aged between four and 25, and provide training and resources to teachers and education providers to enable them to prepare young people for a successful future.

Our enterprise education programmes are underpinned by a guiding principle of 'Learning by Doing'; learning to be enterprising, learning

---

[12] pfeg and EdComs survey, 2011
[13] pfeg and NCB/Panelbase, January 2012

to manage money well, and our flagship Company Programme is mapped by a number of exam boards to their qualifications.

As we lead calls for changes in education policy and welcome announcements such as the Education Secretary's in December 2014, we will continue to deliver high-quality, relevant programmes across the UK, supporting our teachers and encouraging young people to embrace new ways of learning and thinking about their futures.

Tackling the skills gap now and committing to a long-term skills strategy that incorporates the five key skills will ensure young people are ready for the challenge of work when they finish education.

LOCAL HOMES FOR LOCAL PEOPLE

Councillor Tom Hunt, Campaigns Director at Parliament Street and is the Lead Member for Strategic Planning at East Cambridgeshire District Council, explains how Community Land Trusts (CLTs) can make a significant contribution to tackling the housing crisis and helping rural communities remain sustainable.

INTRODUCTION

Without doubt, housing will be one of the key issues going into the next General Election. Despite much heavy lifting by the coalition government, whichever party offers the best policy solutions to what remains a housing crisis will have an electoral edge. For the Conservative Party, a key and unalterable priority should be to do everything we can to help give people a hand onto the property ladder.

One of the reasons why Margaret Thatcher is so admired is because of what she did for working families who wanted to own their home. Before she came to power, 55% of homes were owner-occupied, by the time she left office, the proportion was 66%.

After 13 years of failed Labour planning policy and regional spatial strategies, the crisis when the coalition came to power was acute. The average age of a first time buyer is now 36 and over 40 in some regions, and the average house price is over 7 times the average annual salary. Moreover, rents, especially in the capital are spiralling out of control, and council housing waiting lists are also exploding. In Tower Hamlets it is currently over 24,000.

SMART GOVERNMENT: A PARLIAMENT STREET GUIDE

The coalition government has made notable progress. The Minister of State for Housing & Planning, Brandon Lewis has said that over 700,000 homes have been delivered since May 2010 and that 230,000 permissions have been granted by local councils in the year to June 2014.[14]

What is more, the government's local plan-led system has more often than not empowered local communities, injecting a healthy dose of democracy into the planning system. Around 80% of local authorities have now published a draft local plan, setting out clearly where local development should happen within their areas. Moreover, Neighbourhood Planning has also made strides, over 1,000 have now been adopted across the country and the number continues to grow.

However, there is far more work to do. Although numbers are important in relation to housing, they do not tell the full story. We also need to focus on the quality of the housing built, whether the housing mixes delivered suit local needs as opposed to developer profit motives, and that the resulting increase in housing numbers suits working families who want to move up or onto the property ladder, not only property speculators.

The debates relating to housing and planning, ahead of the drawing up of the party manifestos, are already providing evidence that the debate is moving beyond numbers alone. There is an increasing recognition that a purely free market, planning free for all approach is not working, especially in our nation's capital. The Labour Party has already suggested that it is seriously considering a new policy where 50% of new housing in "housing growth areas" can be reserved for "local" first-time buyers for up to two months to give them priority

---

[14] Brandon Lewis MP, 'Our plan to create thousands of new homeowners', *Conservativehome* 15 Dec 2014

access.[15] Moreover, as an extension of this policy, it is also thought to be considering allowing local councils the power to block new homes being used for buy-to-let.

The feeling is that this policy shift by Labour is driven by a desire to shore up their core vote and see off the UKIP challenge. There is no doubt that if Labour were to follow through on these proposals, there would be some populist appeal to hard pressed working families who currently feel shut out of the property market.

The recent *Conservative Home* manifesto also touches upon this same theme. The manifesto seeks to be rigidly focused on the day-to-day concerns of the average working voter. Hence its three themes: 1. Homes 2. Savings 3. Jobs. It is pleasing that such an influential Conservative voice sees the electoral potential of focusing intensely on voters' day-to-day concerns, and to attempt to come up with solutions to their problems, as opposed to focusing on less tangible metropolitan preoccupations.

The key theme of Labour's housing chapter was to use the power of the state to actively push a pro-ownership planning policy and opportunities to first-time buyers, moving beyond the obsession with numbers. However, as always, one needs to be wary of policy solutions being too top-down. Labour's Lyons Review into housing goes down this route; what we need is recognition that top-down doesn't always work and to create places and the types of homes people actually want. As Conservatives, we need to be alive to the potential of community led housing. Community led housing is the citizen, the people, the community saying what they want.

---

[15] Grice A, 'Labour would reserve half of all new-build homes for 'local' first time buyers, *The Independent* 16 Oct 2014

Although there is much the Conservative led coalition government can be proud of when it comes to housing and planning, we are still far away from where we need to be. The London property market is broken and too often the local planning-led system has been undermined by speculative developers who have sought to circumvent local democracy.

One area where the Conservative Party can lead the new housing agenda is through increased backing of Community Land Trusts. Although numerous housing and planning Ministers have been supportive of CLTs, most notably Grant Shapps MP and Nick Boles MP, the extent to which CLTs have been seen as a truly significant solution to the housing crisis has been limited. CLTs offer the potential to provide genuinely affordable housing, both to rent and to buy for thousands of people, and the Party needs to do more to back them and the local communities that want them.

The CLT concept, born in the USA, actually first made its presence known in Stonesfield, Oxfordshire in 1983. More recently, however, one of the first incarnations of the CLT model was in Rock in Cornwall where house prices and private rents were escalating so rapidly as a result of buyers from elsewhere purchasing second homes that the local community was forced to take action by setting up a CLT to help provide pathways to home ownership for local people.

CLT CASE STUDIES

In East Cambridgeshire, we set up the county's first CLT in the picturesque village of Stretham that lies between Ely and Cambridge. According to property analyst Home Track, property prices in Cambridge have actually grown at a faster rate than in London since the onset of the financial crisis. The average property is now valued at £348,300 – 32.5% higher than its 2007 peak.

The booming science park in Cambridge and the associated growth of the 'Silicon Fen' has meant that many who work in Cambridge have looked to rent or buy outside the city in the surrounding villages which are more affordable. However, one of the negative consequences of this has been that many of the local young people in these villages have struggled to rent and buy affordably as a result of the increased house prices and rents linked to this explosion of the Cambridge property market. Being in work, the vast majority do not qualify for council housing, but also struggle to rent privately, often living with their parents for many years or leaving the area where they were bought up. Tight planning restrictions and opposition to development have also added to this acute shortage of affordable housing.

As a local authority, East Cambridgeshire District Council wants to plan for growth and CLTs, by giving the community genuine influence and control over new development. They are now the preferred way for delivering affordable housing in the district.

Stretham and Wilburton CLT has sought to provide a community-led solution to the problem. Again this has been funded through cross-subsidy. Planning permission was recently granted by East Cambridgeshire District Council for a CLT on open countryside on the edge of the village, on land not allocated in the local plan for market development.

The local community has worked closely with the private house builder Lara Homes who have developed the units. As a result, 35 new market homes will be provided, as well as 15 affordable units that will be managed by the local community through the Stretham and Wilburton CLT. The 15 units will be rented out at rates linked to local incomes and priority will be given to those with a local connection. Those who live in one of the 15 CLT homes can acquire up to 80% of the property. However, if they wish to move on, they cannot sell the home on the open market. It has to be sold back to the CLT.

Councillor Charles Roberts, council member for the Stretham ward and Deputy Leader of East Cambridgeshire District Council is the current Chair and founder of the CLT. Although there have been many challenges along the way, his dream is now becoming a reality:

"Stretham is a village with approximately 1700 inhabitants, located just nine miles from the economic prosperity of Cambridge. There is a strong local community, however, with an increase in property prices the local population feel 'priced out'.

Two recent exception site developments have been built against huge resistance from locals who see no benefit for the community. So, in 2012, the Parish Council led the formation of a 'Community Land Trust' (CLT); an industrial provident society. The CLTs primary objective is to provide opportunities for people who live and work within the community. The CLT searched for land and selected a site outside the building envelope to the West of the village. This site relates well to the settlement and is owned by a Cambridge College, however lying outside the development envelope and with the likelihood of substantial local opposition, the site under normal developing circumstances is unlikely to be considered.

In 2013, the Trust undertook an extensive consultation exercise, which was supported by a substantial grant from the 'Commission for Architecture and the Built Environment'. Specialist consultants reached out to every sector of the community from the school children to the retired. The team established what people valued about the village and what form they would like to see development take.

LOCAL HOMES FOR LOCAL PEOPLE

Support grew quickly for the project with only a few residents living adjacent to the proposed site raising concerns. As joint applicants with the developer/ College the CLT were actively involved in developing and agreeing the design brief. Through group and one-to-one meetings with the concerned residents a compromise was reached by providing a substantial bridleway and open space between existing properties and the new development.

A total of fifty houses are planned with fifteen to be held by the CLT for affordable rent and shared-ownership. In addition, to the fifteen plots the Trust receive land for a Doctor's surgery, some work units, a cemetery extension, and considerable open space as a village green in the centre of the development. The Trust will also receive, in cash, 40% of the uplift in value of the thirty-five private plots. The receipt of free building plots and substantial cash uplift funding model will allow the CLT to provide genuinely affordable rents and shared-ownership opportunities for hard-working local people.

The design of the scheme and the individual homes is revolutionary in so far as the streets are laid out in the form of the existing village with a wide range of individually designed homes many of which are purposefully designed to be extended. The CLT owned homes are spread throughout the development, of generous proportions, and are indistinguishable from the private homes."

Councillor Charles Roberts (founder & chair: Stretham & Wilburton CLT, Deputy Leader: East Cambridgeshire District Council)

As a result of these rents being affordable, breathing space is provided for young local people to save for a deposit which opens up the possibility of eventually owning their own home within the community they have been raised. CLTs provide a pathway to home ownership for many hard working local people who form the backbone of rural communities, often working in roles that allow these communities to thrive.

CLTs work best when they create the right incentives. Although the CLT units in Stretham are for rent (one can acquire an 80% stake) their main strength is their ability through the affordability of rent to make it possible for those who live in CLT units to save a deposit consequently opening up opportunities in terms of future home ownership in the village.

The community is opening up opportunities for young adults and families with a local link to get on the property ladder, and once on that ladder, to keep climbing. It could be that further to providing the CLT units, the local CLT could seek to incentivise those living within them to save for a deposit.

Perhaps a formula could be established locally where, if certain amounts were saved for a deposit every year, a certain fraction could be taken off the rent for that property, incentivising responsible behaviour and the kind of steps that bring the prospect of home ownership closer to those living in the CLT units. Perhaps a time limit could be placed on the length of time a particular family or individual can live in a CLT unit, encouraging them to plan for the future, freeing the CLT unit up for another family, and encouraging CLT units to be viewed as springboards to home ownership, not a permanent arrangement.

To date, the vast majority of CLTs have been in rural areas, however, the National CLT Network recently established the Urban CLT Project which is seeking to increase the number of urban CLTs. To date, there are over 20. The most prominent being the East London CLT.

The London Borough of Tower Hamlets has witnessed rapid population growth in recent years leading to spiralling house prices. The average new property, on the open market, is now over £600,000, an increase of 43% over the last year according to The Guardian,[16] and the housing waiting list is now 24,000. Home ownership is a distant dream and out of reach for too many local people, in work, who have been brought up in the Borough.

The East London Community Land Trust, established this year, has given these aspiring homeowners a lifeline. Gailford Try, the developer, were granted permission to develop 229 market rate units on what had been publicly owned land in Mile End (owned by the Greater London Authority) on the understanding that 23 units, on the site of the old St Clements's Hospital site be transferred over to the new East London Community Land Trust.

Membership of the trust is open to anyone who lives, works or has strong active ties to a social institution in the area. Just £1 buys a share in the not-for-profit company. Membership is not the sole consideration when it comes to allocating a CLT home. An independent panel will decide who gets a home in keeping with the council's housing allocation policy. They will be local people with housing needs but enough income to buy a property.

According to the London estate agents Foxtons the average one-bed flat in the borough costs £301,504 and the average three-bed home costs £441,048. However, the prices of homes within the CLT are permanently pegged to median local incomes, meaning that the homes managed by the trust are affordable in perpetuity. As a consequence, a one-bedroom flat on the St Clements's hospital site is £125,000 and a three-bed home £240,000, opening up home ownership for many low income, working local people who would otherwise have no hope of owning a home in their local area. Once successful in

---

[16] Osborne H, 'Asking house prices in London have risen by £80,000 since January' *The Guardian* 19 May 2014

securing one of these CLT homes, whoever it is who purchases one needs to sign a contract agreeing to sell the home back to the CLT if they wish to leave, meaning that all of the units are forever owned by the CLT, meaning that they will be shielding from inflationary house prices and will be affordable for local people in perpetuity.

The East London CLT certainly has a number of advantages. Young families, responsible, in work, and who have lived in the local area all their lives, are now being granted an opportunity to own a home in their local area. Moreover, as was the case with Stretham & Wilburton CLT, the proposal was able to win the support of the whole community, passing through Tower Hamlets Planning Committee with unanimous cross Party support freeing up the wider development of over 200 market homes.

In both urban and rural settings, CLTs can address housing need. When the National Community Land Trust Network was formed in 2011 there were only a handful of CLTs, there are now approximately 170, it is thought that over 1,000 homes will have been provided through CLTs. Moreover, this is not to mention the market homes, linked to the affordable CLT units through the cross-subsidy formula that have come about as a result of community and council support that would have likely not been there without the CLT component.

CLTs have received support and political backing right across the spectrum. On June 4th 2014, over 130 delegates gathered in Parliament only hours after the Queen's speech that had set out the Government's plan for housing to officially launch the National Community Land Trust Network. The event was sponsored by Chair of the Defence Select Committee, Rory Stewart MP, and was also attended by the Planning Minister at the time Nick Boles MP, both passionate in their support for CLTs.

However, despite the progress that has been made, a number of obstacles remain in the way of the CLT agenda that are preventing it reaching its true potential. CLTs need to be more than small scale, rarefied, feel good projects. They need to be a significant component of the national response to the housing crisis. To do this, a number of steps need to be taken.

Despite the successful launch of the National CLT Network and occasional warm words from relevant Ministers, there still appears to be a lack of widespread awareness of CLTs and the potential that they hold. In February a National Action Day is being launched by the National CLT Network in conjunction with Citizens UK to increase the prominence of the agenda, and a sophisticated lobbying campaign is also being developed for this very reason.

Catherine Harrington is the Director of the National CLT Network and is currently working on a number of recommendations that she hopes the three major political parties will bear in mind when drafting their manifestos.

"CLTs are not the solution to the housing crisis but they have to be a much bigger part of it. The mainstream isn't delivering the volume of homes we need or the homes people want. All political parties are trying to find innovative ways to achieve the levels of new supply that will make a meaningful dent in housing need and demand.

However, it's not just the political parties and the housing sector that say we need more housing. It is communities themselves. Many communities want more housing, and more affordable housing, but housing that works for that community and is actually what local people can afford. That's why more and more communities are setting up CLTs. They offer homes at a price linked to medium income, rather than market values, and are genuinely and permanently affordable for the local community.

SMART GOVERNMENT: A PARLIAMENT STREET GUIDE

Whilst the number of new homes delivered by CLTs to date is dwarfed by the levels of new homes needed in this country, the fact that is sometimes forgotten is that CLTs are actually key to increasingly wider housing supply.

We know that if you give communities genuine influence and control over new housing, and not just 'consultation', they will get behind development and bring other members of the community along with them, instead of opting for the default position of being resistant to change.

East London CLT is working with developers Galliford Try and have taken a complex heritage scheme to planning in half the usual time, and achieved unanimous support at Planning Committee. This was because of community support provided by the CLT.

East Cambridgeshire District Council have chosen CLTs as the preferred method of delivering affordable housing in the district, after failing to see community support for rural affordable housing delivered by conventional methods. What we need now is for the political parties to see the potential for CLTs and community-led housing to the wider housing supply agenda and give the sector and these communities the support and prominence they deserve.

Catherine Harrington (Director, National Community Land Trust Network,

The National Community Land Trust Network is working on their own manifesto ahead of the General Election, containing a number of key "asks" from central Government. Of the listed asks, I think the Conservative Party ought to seriously consider the following four "key asks":

RECOMMENDATIONS

A dedicated funding stream for community-led housing in every future Government Affordable Homes Programme. The Home and Communities Agency recently released their prospectus for the 2015-2018 Affordable Homes Programme, the funding for which amounts to over £3 billion. There is no specific funding set aside for community-led housing. This needs to change.

The 2011-2015 Affordable Homes Programme included a £25m pot for community-led housing, for which the National Network lobbied. However, the current 2015-2018 programme has no such funding and, as such, CLTs have to access the main programme and compete for funding.

Encourage local authorities to set up 'local housing revolving loan funds', to provide accessible short-term development finance to community-led housing groups and SME builders. The fund would work by councils using the Second Homes Council Tax, New Homes Bonus or borrowing from the public works loan board, to lend to community-led housing groups and SME builders, just as they have done in Cornwall, and with significant success. However, for local authorities to be able to do this, we are also calling for the borrowing cap for local authorities to be extended.

All new affordable housing in Garden Cities and urban extensions to be vested in a Community Land Trust. With the government's announcement in December 2014 regarding plans for a 13,000 home New Market Town in Bicester, Oxfordshire, it is becoming increasingly clear that whatever Party is in power, New Market Towns are likely to play a significant role in meeting the country's housing need. Like CLTs, the original Garden Cities had trusts that owned and managed the assets and any uplift in land value has been for community benefit and not for private gain. There should be a requirement that 100% of affordable homes are vested in a CLT, to ensure that the homes remain permanently affordable.

A presumption in favour of communities on public authority and local authority land. Communities have not been effectively integrated into public land disposal plans and thus have had to make an invidious choice of selecting one of the bidders for the site. However, this has been a risky process for the community group, taking up considerable volunteer time and financial resources that are potentially abortive.

Although the East London CLT can now be judged as a success story, it was almost eight years in the making and the tendering process was extremely protracted. Initially the East London CLT bid was rejected. They went into partnership with a private developer, drew up detailed plans, but were unsuccessful in the bidding process; the procurement panel opted for Galiford Try. As it happens, Galiford Try were willing to go back to the drawing board with East London CLT and agreed for there to be a CLT element. However fresh plans needed to be drawn up that further delayed the delivery of new affordable homes.

There ought to be a presumption in favour of communities to avoid such delays in the future. National Good Practice Guidance on procurement of public land requires for a presumption in favour of the involvement of communities in the disposal and development of public land and assets, where there is a registered community-led-housing group that can meet local housing need or demand.

Formation of an All Party Parliamentary Group (APPG) on Community Led Development. There needs to be greater recognition of the potential of CLTs to deliver the country's housing needs. The formation of an APPG could make a significant contribution to inserting the CLT agenda into the wider housing debate.

CONCLUSIONS

For me, there are four key reasons why, as Conservatives, we should support CLTs, both locally and nationally. They deliver community led affordable housing for working families that are struggling to continue living within the rural communities where they work and have been raised. Moreover, due to being community led, and leading to results that clearly benefit the settled community, as well as fulfilling an unmet housing need, CLT housing schemes are likely to win the support of the whole community in a way that the ordinary development applications on land outside the development envelope would not.

In the case of Stretham, not only have 15 CLT units been provided, but also 35 market homes. These would not have come about without the CLT element which won over the community. Therefore, CLTs should also be viewed as a mechanism of freeing up development in rural areas more generally, and playing a key role in meeting the housing challenge.

As demonstrated through the Stretham case study, CLT-led applications also lead to good quality, well thought out homes and communities. Both the CLT units and the market component of the development will not be identikit homes. They have been designed by the community for the community.

In the case of urban CLTs, as in rural examples, community support has been won for significant development. Moreover a number of affordable units have been provided to local people to help them remain in their local area. However, what is clear is that the challenges faced by rural and urban CLTs differ, and the approach and model really do need to be led locally.

Important also is the need to balance increasing opportunities for local people to remain living locally, while respecting and encouraging the aspirational urge to climb the property ladder.

Taken as a whole, CLTs offer the potential for the very real tension between the need to provide housing and cater for new communities to be balanced with the responsibility to respect local democracy and the needs of existing communities. Stretham is a rural community that has historically been very anti-development, as demonstrated by the recent Mereham campaign.[17]

How refreshing that the CLT application passed with the overwhelming support of the local community. So much so, that many are now calling for a phase two to provide an extra 20 homes. Providing housing for local people and respecting local democracy need not be mutually exclusive.

CLTs offer great potential. Used and promoted in the right way, they can make a significant contribution towards tackling the housing crisis!

---

[17] Gray L, 'New town refused planning permission', *The Telegraph* 30 Aug 2008

TIME FOR A DOSE OF EURO-REALISM

Shaun Bailey, Former Conservative Parliamentary Candidate for Hammersmith and Special Adviser to the Prime Minister, and Nabil Najjar, Managing Director of Delta Strategies Limited argue that, in today's globalised world, there is more that unites Europe than divides it, and that Britain's place remains within a reformed EU.

INTRODUCTION

No issue has divided British Conservatives throughout recent history more than that of Britain's relationship with the European Union. Ever since the Conservative Prime Minister Ted Heath instigated Britain's membership in 1973, our Party has been at loggerheads as to how best approach the subject. This disagreement and discord came to a head during the Premiership of John Major, and his support for the Maastricht Treaty and the closer European ties it heralded, eventually caused a rebellion across the Party which forced Major to resign and re-stand for the leadership, ultimately winning.

Following the Party's defeat in 1997, the issue broadly subsided until recent times, when further integration following the Lisbon Treaty of 2007, coupled with the rapid expansion of the Union caused some to question whether continued membership of the EU and the consequences it led to, including increased net migration into the UK, were in fact worthwhile. Today, it seems both public opinion and the conservative family are very much divided on our future within the Union, and the 'Euro-sceptic' wing of the Party has continued to gather momentum. With a referendum on our membership proposed for 2017 should the Conservatives win the upcoming election, we stand on the cusp of a historic impasse. Although it is tempting to side with the sceptics and revert back within our borders, we risk alienating ourselves from our geographical, political, cultural and economic allies at precisely the time when we need unity. This is not about Europhobia versus Europhilia: it is about Euro-realism – understanding the fact that we are in, whether we like it or not, and that disassociating from the Union will not change that, and analysing the position functionally as opposed to ideologically. That is not to say that we must accept the Union as it is. Changes must occur, but to flagrantly abandon the Union at such a volatile time is not in our best interests, and nor does it send the right message.

THAT WHICH UNITES US IS GREATER THAN THAT WHICH DIVIDES

The simple reality is that the United Kingdom is forever tied to Europe, and, should we leave the European Union; that will not change. Our shared history, culture and ideals, coupled with our geographical proximity and our intertwined economies and defences will forever connect us with our European neighbours, whether we remain in the Union or not. In an unpredictable, volatile and dangerous world, in which new threats emerge constantly, we are strongest when we stand together with the rest of our continent.

Never has this been clearer than during the recent terrorist attacks that occurred across France in January 2015. The tragic murders which took place across Paris served as a shocking reminder of the dangers we face, but what was even more striking was the way Europe came together in the aftermath of the event. David Cameron stood alongside Francois Hollande, Angela Merkel, Helle Thorning-Schmidt and other European and world leaders in a stunning display of solidarity and unity in the face of a barbaric enemy. Our shared values and commitment to freedom, equality and liberty shone through the darkness and made clear the fact that we are strongest when we stand together, and that only by working together with our allies will we best defend ourselves against these threats.

Even if we did leave the European Union, our defence and security will still be tied to Europe through our membership of NATO, meaning we will retain military ties with France, Germany, Italy, Spain and many other EU states. The caveats of the Treaty mean Britain will need to stand with the other signatories in the event of an attack, so that even if we do leave the EU, our fate will remain tied to that of our neighbours.

Now is not the time to withdraw within our own borders, but rather the time to boldly embrace the bonds which unite us, and understand that what happens next-door could well happen to us. We must work together to tackle the challenges we face, be they Islamic extremism, cyber-security or any one of the other dangers staring us in the face.

THE ECONOMICS OF AN EXIT

Since 1994, trade between the United Kingdom and the European Union has exceeded 50% of the UK's total international trade. This sounds significant, but the scale of this dependence becomes even more poignant when one takes into account the fact that, in 2012, non-EU OECD (Organisation for Economic Co-operation and Development) countries, including the United States of America, Australia, Canada, Mexico and Japan, accounted for just below 20% of total trade; only slightly more than the figure accrued through trade with IMF emerging economies which equated to 14%.[18]

Clearly the trade facilitated by the European Union is fundamental to the British economy, and as with any organisation, membership comes at a cost, although that cost is often significantly overestimated by sceptics. In return for access to a free and integrated market worth over £400bn per annum, Britain gave the EU roughly €14.5bn in 2013. Notwithstanding the fact that UK farmers received €3.1bn in subsidies, researchers received over €1bn in grants and total EU expenditure on the UK exceeded €6.3bn that same year, this seems a comparably small price to pay.[19]

This does not even begin to take into account the job opportunities created within the UK as a direct result of the EU. Our enviable position allows us to offer business access to the largest single market in the world, without the need to sign up to a shared currency, creating an ideal environment for businesses to thrive. Should we leave the EU, the numerous major global corporations who develop and export from the UK across the Union would be faced with significant tariffs when exporting products, and may subsequently leave, costing jobs and tax revenue. Several commentators predict that companies such as Airbus will move their operations to Germany or France, and the numerous car companies which produce vehicles in the UK will move to lower-cost countries within the EU.[20]

When combined, the economic costs of leaving the Union are potentially massive, but there are those who seem to think that we

---

[18] Springford J and Tilford S, *The Great British Trade-Off*, Centre for European Reform, 2014
[19] Vinter R, 'How much do we give the EU, and how much do we get back', *London loves Business*, 21 Oct 2014
[20] 'If Britain leaves Europe, we will become a renegade without economic power', *The Guardian*, 18 Nov 2012

will be able to have the best of both worlds. They claim that we will be able to close our borders to our neighbours, renege on our support of the EU's institutions and still retain access to the free market.

It is highly unlikely that France, Germany and the other leading EU nations will accept a 'pick and mix' approach, as evidenced by the reluctance of other member states to allow the UK any flexibility around the Social Chapter of the Maastricht Treaty. Instead, it is far more likely that the UK will need to adopt an approach not dissimilar to that of Norway, and retain membership of the European Economic Area (EEA) – not without significant cost. As it is outside the Union, certain Norwegian products are subject to high EU import tariffs, and subsequent Norwegian counter-tariffs on EU products have led to them becoming very expensive for ordinary Norwegian citizens – French cheese, for example, is subject to an import tax of 400%.

Their lack of input on EU policy is also a problem for Norway – the Head of the Bergen Chamber of Commerce, Marit Warncke, told the Telegraph that *"We are the most obedient of EU members, rapidly implementing directives to the letter, yet we have no say in them. We are sitting outside in the corridors, instead of being at the decision table."* [21] Equally, Norway, despite having no membership or voting rights within the EU, still contributes several hundred million Euros per annum. When extrapolated, that would equate to a UK bill of roughly €2bn per annum to follow the Norwegian model [22]

Unlike Norway whose relationship with the EU has evolved organically over time, it is hard to imagine the EU member states retaining the same modicum of goodwill towards the UK following an

---

[21] Alexander H, 'Is Norway's EU example really an option for Britain?' *The Telegraph* 08 July 2012.
[22] Ibid

acrimonious exit from the Union, so it is reasonable to expect the costs of retaining economic privileges to be significantly higher.

So the question remains – if we do indeed leave the EU, how will we compensate for the significant trade deficit that will inevitably occur? Euro-sceptics have put forward a handful of alternatives, but one of the consistent favourites, both in print and in conversation, is that we can tap into our links with the Commonwealth nations, and by boosting trade with these countries, we can make up for the shortfall caused by the exit – but this invites a further question – 'can the Commonwealth really cover the cost?'.

CAN THE COMMONWEALTH REALLY COVER THE COST?

One of the most consistent claims peddled by our Party's Euro-sceptics is that we can cover the net loss of trade associated with an exit from the European Union through bolstering trade with the Commonwealth. They often point to the fact that, to date, there has never been a formal trade agreement across its member states, and that, by forging stronger links with the Commonwealth, the UK will more than compensate for the loss of EU trade. Although this rhetoric serves as an easy answer when questions arise around the economic drawbacks of exiting the EU, the simple reality is that is misguided. Firstly, the theory that retaining European trading links and developing new links with the Commonwealth are mutually exclusive concepts is a fallacy, and secondly, the idea that we can replace the £151bn of EU export and £218bn of EU import trade[23] we enjoyed in 2013 with additional Commonwealth trade is highly suspect.

---

[23] 'UK Overseas Trade Statistics with EU: January 2014', *HM Revenue and Customs, 2014*

TIME FOR A DOSE OF EURO-REALISM

In fact, since the London Declaration of 1949, the United Kingdom has spearheaded the Commonwealth of Nations, one of the primary purposes of which is the facilitation of free inter-Commonwealth trade, and this connection has allowed us access to that market since that date. In 1997, a report commissioned by the Commonwealth Secretariat found that, despite the absence for formalised treaties, Commonwealth nations enjoyed a 'cost advantage' when trading amongst each other, and furthermore, overhead costs of inter-member trading were reduced by as much as 15% when compared to comparable trade with non-member nations.[24]

This is not to say that the Commonwealth has been utilised to its maximum capacity, and of course there is always scope for increased trade across its membership. Yet this does not need to occur at the expense of our highly profitable relationship with the EU. In fact, in 2013, a trade agreement was signed between the EU and Canada, which is worth over £1.3bn per annum to British businesses and our economy,[25] further reinforcing the fact that we can hone relationships with the Commonwealth both independently and in unison with our economic partners across Europe. The Commonwealth is a worthy and viable trading partner, but the claim that boosting our trade relationship with it will plug the black hole that leaving the EU will create, is unsubstantiated.

The Deputy Secretary-General of the Commonwealth, responsible for Political Affairs, Masire Mwamba, made clear the fact that the organisation should not be seen as an alternative to the EU during an event at the Houses of Parliament in early 2014. She emphasised that the Commonwealth is a loose and free organisation not bound by

---

[24] Lundan S ad Jones G, 'The Commonwealth Effect and the Process of Internationalisation', *The World Economy* 24/1 2001 pp.99-118
[25] *Department for Business, Innovation and Skills,* 18 Oct 2013

treaties, and that it should not be viewed in competition with the EU. She said that there should be 'no conversation around the Commonwealth replacing the European Union', and argued that the UK can leverage its position within the Commonwealth to deliver meaningful trade with other members, but that it will never take the place of the EU.[26]

CAN WE 'SPLIT THE DIFFERENCE'?

The European Union is far from perfect, but we are better off in than out. Rather than jumping ship and risking an economic backlash, we should take the lead in rebuilding a more competitive, democratic and effective union. If the Conservatives are returned to power in May 2015, either as part of another coalition, or with the majority so badly craved, David Cameron will have to go about his attempted renegotiation with haste, with the prospect of an In-Out Referendum looming only two years away. He will need to leave the negotiating table with enough of a compromise so as to placate the moderate Euro-sceptics; and in doing so, place the 'In' campaign in a position to argue that the benefits outweigh the costs.

The European Union, with its multifaceted agenda, is not a binary organisation. It is not entirely a case of 'in or out', and as John Major showed during the Maastricht negotiations, clever negotiation can allow a government to moderate the extent to which it must abide by the Union's social policy restrictions. David Cameron himself has shown willingness to confront the EU-juggernaut on a handful occasions, when the stakes were particularly high. In early 2013, he played a leading role in

---

[26] Masire Mwamba in conversation with London Conservative Future, 26 March 2014

securing the first EU budget cut in its fifty six year history – and not an insignificant one either, with the total amount saved in the region of €80bn.[27] He fought back once more to flatly reject the £1.7bn 'bill' issued by the EU in response to the UK's improved economic performance. By categorically rejecting the instruction, and negotiating effectively, that bill was eventually halved to little over £850m – still expensive, but a drop in the ocean when taken against the economic benefits Britain enjoys from its membership.

David Cameron will need to step up once again, and use his political leverage to barter for a more effective Union. He will have allies – Angela Merkel herself has expressed concern at Britain's proposed exit from the EU. It is fair to say that Germany will not wish to remain the sole economic powerhouse in the Union, at a time where the shared currency they themselves are tied into faces repeated battering as its various expenders suffer economic difficulty. The election of Syriza in Greece will do nothing to allay these concerns. Cameron will also be able to tap into the European Conservatives and Reformists Party, the anti-federalist political group in the European Parliament founded under his leadership of the Conservative Party. This grouping now houses seventy two MEPs from fifteen countries, and is the third largest political group in the European Parliament. Between them, there should be enough clout to deliver some degree of repatriated powers to the United Kingdom.

With clever negotiation, a series of concessions can be secured. Perhaps the most politically important will be the ability to curb the free movement of peoples across the European Union. Free movement of peoples is a founding tenet of the European ideal,

---

[27] Chapman J, 'Cameron wins historic cut in EU's spending', *Daily Mail*, 8 Feb 2013

and as such, it is unrealistic to expect that the UK will see control over its borders repatriated. David Cameron has, however, already indicated that he will push for the power to curb migrant welfare, calling it 'an absolute requirement in renegotiation'.[28] There is some debate about whether such a concession will require formal treaty change, and if so, whether referenda must be held across member states, but, in principle, this is achievable. If we can reduce the financial incentives traditionally associated with inter-EU migration to the UK, we can limit the number of immigrants at a local, more casual level. Measures such as withholding 'in work' benefits and social housing until an EU worker has been in the UK for four years, and stopping child benefits for the children of EU workers living elsewhere in Europe should go some way towards reducing the flow of migrants.

Secondly, the Conservatives have already put forwards plans to limit the enforceability of rulings from the European Court of Human Rights (ECHR). Under proposals to be included in the coming manifesto, the British Parliament will be given power to veto ECHR judgments, curtailing its power and repatriating sovereignty to Westminster.[29] Justice Secretary Chris Grayling has gone even further, pledging to replace the EU-wide Human Rights Act, with a British Bill of Rights. Whilst this pledge has been made before, ahead of the 2010 General Election, this time, the pressure will be on to deliver it, and amid the broader debate on European membership, it is likely that it will come to pass. This will allow the UK to mould its own, bespoke charter of codified rights for its citizens, accountable to British lawmakers and courts, and free

---

[28] Maclellan K, 'Cameron tells EU – let us curb migrant welfare, or risk EU leaving', *Reuters* 28 Nov 2014
[29] Bowcott O, 'Conservatives pledge powers to ignore ECHR rulings', *The Guardian* 3 Oct 2014

from the interference of European Union bureaucracy. Finally, a move to strip back some of the excrescent encroachments of EU policy, including fisheries policy and Common Agricultural Policy (CAP) and ensuring that the UK no longer heavily subsidises redistributive funds such as the Cohesion Fund will help level the playing field.

As well as pulling back, there are steps we can take to reform the European Union from within. We should take the lead in trying to maximise efficiency and ensure the EU becomes more competitive on the global stage. By leading the campaign to unshackle the European workforce, to cut red tape and to deregulate financial markets, we can set about building an effective, competitive European Union from within.

CONCLUSIONS

A recent poll by Comres and OpenEurope found that, a referendum over EU membership under the current terms would see 41% of participants vote to leave and 37% vote to stay (20% undecided). However, should 'a new settlement' be reached, 32% would vote to leave, versus 47% to stay (18% undecided).[30] Clearly, the public is keen to see the goalposts shifted but do not wish to sever ties entirely.

If we can achieve a renegotiation which repatriates a degree of judicial authority, limits the amount we pay out into redistributive and collective schemes, and allows us a degree of control over our borders, that should be enough to placate the moderate Euro-sceptics. These migratory, judicial and social amendments to our

---

[30] Comres and OpenEurope polling, May 2013

relationship with the Union will place the UK in a healthier position. We need to establish what we can achieve both in terms of spearheading changes where possible, and repatriating powers where necessary, we can move towards a Euro-realistic approach to dealing with the EU. If we can achieve this, whilst at the same time ensuring that we retain access to the significant economic benefits the EU provides, then we will have achieved a sustainable, mutually beneficial and positive renegotiation with – enough to make most of the UK population comfortable enough that they will vote to remain within the single biggest market in the world.

ISLAMIC EXTREMISM: THE GREATEST THREAT TO BRITAIN'S FUTURE

Clare George-Hilley, a Public Affairs Director and Head of Research for Parliament Street, outlines how we have allowed religious extremism a free reign for too long, and makes recommendations to the Government on how to counter it.

INTRODUCTION

Britain has long been the home of tolerance and equal opportunity for people from all walks of life. We are the country that defeated Nazi Germany, ridding the world of one of the greatest evils known to man, proudly upholding liberty and never giving in to tyranny, no matter what the cost.

Our forefathers gave their lives so that our generation can live in peace and enjoy freedoms that are now so commonplace that we almost take them from granted. Many hundreds of thousands of people have travelled to Britain to make it their home; their culture and diversity enriching our society as well as enhancing our economy.

Yet it is in this climate of tolerance that is so recognisable in the British way of life, that we have allowed intolerance to flourish behind the scenes. Under the guise of free speech and respect for other cultures, the evils of Islamic extremism have been able to fester unchallenged. We have in many ways been the architects of our own misfortune, allowing extremism to gain a foothold in different levels of society.

The warning signs have been there for many years, but we chose to ignore them. From gender segregation in Islamic schools to alarming protests where extremists waved signs declaring 'behead those who insult Islam' without fear of arrest, Britain has been sleep-walking into the hands of extremists for the last decade.

THE PROBLEM

It is no surprise that our schools have been infiltrated as part of the Trojan Horse plot in Birmingham. In one school, facilities were used to copy and produce DVDs of Osama Bin Laden's training videos and children were addressed by Sheikh Shady al-Suleiman, a fundamentalist preacher who has called on God to "destroy the enemies of Islam."[31]

Many hundreds of extremists have packed their bags and travelled to Syria and Iraq to torture, to maim and to behead innocent people.[32] The extent of their psychotic behaviour can be seen in their use of social media to glorify and to celebrate murder and brutality.

For many years, under the last Labour government, openly preaching hatred on the streets of Britain went unpunished. Abu Hamza, for example, spent months defying the authorities and enjoying taxpayer funding of his vicious agenda, which poisoned the minds of young Muslims without anybody able to stop him. Finally, under the Conservatives, he was extradited and jailed in the United States on charges of terrorism, but the fact that this dangerous criminal had evaded justice for so long is in itself a scandal.

In Rotherham, gangs of young men were systematically abusing underage girls, again without fear of arrest. An independent report by Professor Alexis Jay revealed the true extent of the abuse, and

---

[31] Ware J, 'The plot to Islamise Birmingham's schools' *Standpoint* Sept 2014
[32] Wintour P and Watt N, 'Up to 400 British citizens may be fighting in Syria, says William Hague' *The Guardian* 16 June 2014

ISLAMIC EXTREMISM: THE GREATEST THREAT TO BRITAIN'S FUTURE

highlighted the Police, Council and local government agencies failure to take action. The report concluded that "…the collective failures of political and officer leadership were blatant," yet there were no real punishments for the men who abused thousands of children.[33]

Much of the material covered in the report was too shocking to print in the press. Children were raped by multiple perpetrators, trafficked to other towns and cities in the north of England, abducted, beaten, and intimidated.

Another was doused in petrol and threatened with being set alight, some were threatened with guns and others were forced to witness rape and warned they would be next. Another child in the report, known only as 'H' was found drunk in the back of a car with a suspected abuser, who had indecent photos of her on his phone – she was just 12 years old.

You may think such horrific incidents were impossible in modern Britain, but you would be wrong. These threats are regular, active and growing, and underline the problem that we have created for ourselves by allowing extremism to flourish in our country. They were happening then, and they are almost certainly happening now.

The left's solution to the problem is to brand anyone who dares confront it as 'racist' instead of taking action on a crisis that risks putting the British way of life at risk. After the murder of soldier Lee Rigby on the streets of Britain, the public no longer buy into the left's argument that we should sit back and shut up in the face of Islamic extremism. The public want tangible action and answers, and the left's usual defence of extremist practices has finally run out of steam.

If we wish to drain the swamp of hatred which is polluting our country, we must ensure engagement with moderate Muslims and do

---

[33] Jay A, *Independent Inquiry into Child Sexual Exploitation in Rotherham (1997 – 2013)*, 2014

more to help them root out terror and prevent extremism from gaining a foothold. The positive example they set must be taken and projected across the whole of the UK, to capture the imagination of the young and make embarking on the road to extremism impossible and more importantly, immoral.

Eric Pickles, the Communities Secretary, received much criticism from the Muslim Council of Britain when he wrote a letter calling on Imams to, "explain and demonstrate how faith in Islam can be part of British identity".[34] Despite the name calling, Pickles was right, and those who are serious about ridding our country of extremism will be helping, not hindering his efforts.

His letter continued, "We must show our young people, who may be targeted, that extremists have nothing to offer them. We must show them that there are other ways to express disagreement, that their right to do so is dependent on the very freedoms that extremists seek to destroy."

These were wise words from a Minister seeking to ensure that moderate Muslims are empowered to tell a positive message about Islam and can help young, impressionable people practise their religion peacefully. Such cohesive activity will ensure that negative perceptions about Islam amongst the British people are tackled and that young people will no longer be preyed upon by those seeking to indoctrinate and radicalise for their own twisted ideology.

NEXT STEPS

There are three 'next steps' that Britain must take if it wishes to win the war against Islamic extremism, which is without doubt a huge threat to the freedoms which we all hold dear. There is no single

---

[34] Pickles E, Open letter to Imams, 2014

ISLAMIC EXTREMISM: THE GREATEST THREAT TO BRITAIN'S FUTURE

solution to this problem, but, by working together, we will find that solution to overcome it.

The first is to work with Muslim leaders in mosques and other organisations to make it clear that Islam totally rejects violence and that those who go down that path have no place within the religion, or in Britain. This requires moderate Muslims to speak up louder than the extremists, with full government and public backing, to ensure that the narrative is not hijacked by those who wish to do us harm. Muslim leaders in Britain need to feel empowered and supported when they speak out, and we should do everything in our power to enable them to do so.

The second is to come down much harder on extremism. It is a national scandal that Britain is one of the leading suppliers of terrorists to Syria. We have to ask ourselves what is happening to our country when this is the case. But then again, when we allow our schools to be transformed into mini-training camps and enable preachers to spread hatred openly, what else should we expect? The recent rush of recruits heading out to commit unspeakable atrocities grew up in modern Britain and it is therefore clear that this can no longer be tolerated. Passports should be seized and perhaps more importantly, family members and friends should be properly questioned to find out exactly how much individuals knew. It is the only way to gather the necessary intelligence and prevent further atrocities.

The third and final step is for the Muslim community to become more proactive in rooting out extremism. Often when an atrocity has been committed it is easier to stay quiet than it is to speak up and condemn, for fear of unnecessary and unfair association. But in a modern, free Britain, the public should provide total support for Imams and other leaders who are doing their best to prevent and condemn terrorist activity and to keep our country safe.

Whatever our challenges, Britain remains a strong, tolerant and fair country, where people of all faiths and indeed views are welcomed, but we cannot afford to allow our culture of freedom to become an escalator for those who wish to do us, and others, harm. For too long we have allowed jihadists to fund their illegal activities on a life of benefits and preach hatred without being properly reprimanded by the Police.

We have fought many wars at home and overseas in our quest to maintain our values and keep our country and others safe. We have overcome great evils against all odds and upheld the flame of liberty and freedom despite our darkest days.

Working together, Britain will overcome and at last rid itself of Islamic extremism, but our failure to tackle this serious problem wherever and whenever it occurs will mean that task may take decades instead of years.

NEW ENERGY, NEW JOBS

Aisha Vance, Director of Energy and Security, Parliament Street, and Dr. James P. Verdon, MA (Cantab), M.Sci, Ph.D, BGS Senior Research Fellow in Geophysics, School of Earth Sciences, University of Bristol argue that implementing a US-style energy policy will benefit us as much as it has our cousins across the pond.

In 2009 the US was in the deepest recession since the 1920s,' unemployment was over 10% and former companies that were the foundation of American industry had begun to collapse. The US lost over 7.5 million jobs and entire states went into huge debt in its wake.[35] Around the same time the shale-gas boom was about to begin, a technique called Hydraulic Fracturing or 'Fracking' was about to become the white-knight of America's economy.

In hard-hit states like Pennsylvania and the other states along the east coast, Fracking has benefited their local economy, and has created 1.7 million new direct and indirect jobs in the United States.[36] Some reports say it is likely to rise over 3 million, when it is projected the US will overtake Saudi Arabia in oil output.[37]

The shale gas boom has added $62 billion to federal and state treasuries, with that total expected to rise to $111 billion by 2020. By 2035, U.S. oil and natural gas operations could provide more than $5 trillion in cumulative capital expenditures to the economy, while

---

[35] Zuckerman M, 'The Great Jobs Recession goes on' *US News* 11 Feb 2011
[36] Efstathiou J, 'Fracking will support 1.7 million jobs, study shows' *Bloomberg,* 23 Oct 2012.
[37] *The State of American Energy,* American Petroleum Institute (API) , 2013

generating more than $2.5 trillion in cumulative additional government revenues.[38]

Although the game-changing technology has been used since the early 1940s in the US and Canada, it wasn't until the recession hit, and oil prices sky-rocketed that oil companies began to invest heavily into the technology. The revolution of the shale gas boom led to the satisfaction of a large portion of US demand through domestic production rather than reliance on OPEC oil. Moreover, fracking has allowed the US to become vastly energy independent and less reliant on oil and gas from the Middle East, Russia and Venezuela.

In the UK, only two companies, iGas Energy and Cuadrilla, have made attempts to drill. You'd be excused if you thought there were many more companies drilling all over the countryside, when in fact there are only four sites that have drilled in the UK. The process for gaining permits for hydraulic fracturing can be long and drawn out, with investors often having to patiently wait for years while community engagement takes place, which is often infiltrated with relentless scare-mongering PR tactics from environmental groups like Greenpeace.

The Department of Energy and Climate Change estimates that by 2025 the UK will have to import more than 70% of its energy consumption, assuming we do not utilise shale gas. Moreover, the exploration of gas will mean new high-paying jobs for men and women up and down the countryside. The Institute of Directors estimated that UK shale gas production would be a huge benefit to the economy, including a benefit to public finances, attracting investment of £3.7 billion and support of up to 74,000 jobs directly, indirectly and through broader economic stimulus.[39]

---

[38] Ibid
[39] *Developing Onshore Shale Gas and Oil'*, DECC, Dec 2013

A BRIEF HISTORY OF HYDRAULIC FRACTURING (FRACKING)

The oil and gas industry has long known that the presence of fractures in the reservoir rock mass will allow hydrocarbon to flow more easily into the well, improving production rates. While fractures occur naturally, from the earliest days of the industry, operators have sought methods to create man-made fractures in the rocks they were targeting.

In 1865, Colonel Edward A.L. Roberts, a veteran of the US Civil War, received a patent for a "nitroglycerin torpedo" that could be inserted into an oil well and detonated to create fractures in the rock. Colonel Roberts was able to improve production rates by as much as 1000% in some cases. The technique of 6 "well-shooting" – using explosives to generate fractures in reservoir rocks – reached its zenith with the Project Gasbuggy tests in New Mexico in 1967. As part of Operation Plowshare, the push to find peaceful alternative uses for nuclear weapons, the US Department of Energy detonated a 29 kiloton nuclear device at a depth of 4,240 feet below ground in a tight, low permeability gas reservoir. The explosion successfully fractured the reservoir, and production tests showed a substantial increase in gas production. However, this gas was found to be contaminated by radioactive tritium, and the project was soon shelved.[40]

Instead, the use of explosives to fracture reservoir rocks was being superseded by a newer, more efficient technology: by 1947, Stanolind Oil had identified that fractures could be created by pumping fluids at high pressure into a formation. Stanolind performed the first such hydraulic fracture stimulation at a gas field in Kansas, using 1,000 gallons of gelled gasoline as the fracturing fluid. By 1949, over 300

---

[40] US Dept. of Energy Legacy Management, *Gasbuggy, New Mexico, Site Fact Sheet*

wells had been "stimulated" in this manner,[41] and the technique of hydraulic fracturing soon became a common tool in the conventional oil and gas industry. The American Petroleum Institute estimates that over one million oil and gas wells have been hydraulically stimulated.[42]

HORIZONTAL DRILLING

There is more to shale gas extraction than hydraulic fracturing. An equally crucial technology, without which shale gas would not be commercially viable, is the ability of drillers to turn wellbores to run horizontally along the shale layers. This horizontal drilling allows a much larger volume of rock to be accessed from one small well pad. Horizontal drilling was first developed in the 1930s, but became widely commercially used only in the 1980s. The Wytch Farm oil field underneath Poole Harbour was a pioneer in the use of extended reach lateral wells.[43] [44]

THE BARNETT SHALE

In the wake of the 1970s energy crisis a Texan oilman George Mitchell began looking to extract gas from the Barnett Shale, a shale formation underlying some of his existing conventional fields in northeast Texas. The fact that shale rocks contained abundant hydrocarbon resources was well known. However, conventional wisdom dictated that the low permeability of shale would prevent commercial extraction.

---

[41] Montgomery C.T. and Smith M.B. 'Hydraulic fracturing: History of an enduring technology' *Journal of Petroleum Technology*, Dec 2010, pp26-32
[42] API, *Hydraulic Fracturing Q & A's*
[43] Mantle K, 'The art of controlling wellbore trajectory' *Schlumberger Oilfield Review 25*, 2010, pp.54-55
[44] Energy Information Administration, 'Drilling sideways – A review of horizontal well technology and its domestic application' 1993

In almost 20 years of experimentation to unlock these rocks, a crucial breakthrough pioneered by Mitchell Energy was a change in the composition of the fracturing fluid. In conventional reservoirs, large amounts of chemicals were typically added to the fluid to create a viscous gel, along with breakers to break down the gel once it had penetrated the formation. Instead, Mitchell Energy began using a large volume of water, but a relatively small amount of additives. Typically, the principal component was a friction reducer, so the new style frac fluid has become known as "slick-water", as opposed to the "gel fracs" used previously.[45] Mitchell Energy found that the lower amount of additives required for a slick-water frac reduced costs while substantially improving production.[46][47]

In the late 1990s, using slick-water fracs in combination with horizontal wells, Mitchell Energy began to produce commercial volumes of gas from the Barnett Shale. Soon, competitors were following the same approach, looking for acreage in the Barnett Shale, as well as targeting other shale formations across North America. The shale gas revolution had begun.

THE HYDRAULIC FRACTURING PROCESS

Energy companies in the UK also investigated using the same approach; but the process is very technical and therefore easy to misunderstand.

The aim of hydraulic fracturing is to create fractures that connect the well bore to the hydrocarbon-bearing rock mass. Typically, the weight of overlying rock

---

[45] Halliburton Fact Sheet H05667: Fracturing fluid systems.
[46] Davids Hinton D. 'The seventeen-year overnight wonder' *Journal of American History 99*, 2012, pp. 229-235
[47] Wang Z. and Krupnick A. 'A retrospective review of shale gas development in the United States': *Resources for the Future Discussion Paper* 2013.

means that stresses acting on a rock mass are compressive. To break the rock, tensile stresses must be created. This can be done by increasing the pore pressure of fluids in the rock such that they exceed the compressive stresses. Once the tensile stress exceeds the tensile strength of the rock, then fractures can be generated.

The hydraulic fractures will develop on planes that are perpendicular to the minimum stress orientation. In most sedimentary basins, the orientation of the minimum compressive stress is horizontal. Therefore the hydraulic stimulation will create vertically orientated fractures that propagate in a direction parallel to the maximum horizontal stress. Most sedimentary formations are layered horizontally. This stratification tends to act as a barrier to fracture propagation. As such, the fractures tend to propagate horizontally along the maximum stress direction, as opposed to vertically.

CONVENTIONAL HORIZONTAL DRILLING

The first stage of the hydraulic fracturing process is to drill a well down to the target shale layer, turning the wellbore horizontally to run along the target zone. The well is then cased and cemented with multiple layers of steel piping. The well must then be perforated in the production zone to allow fluids to pass from the reservoir rocks into the well. A "perforation gun" is lowered into the well, which carries a number of shaped explosive charges. These are detonated to perforate a series of holes in the casing through which fluids can flow. All of the above activity is no different to operations in a conventional well.

HYDRAULIC STIMULATION

Once the well has been drilled, it can be hydraulically stimulated. This is usually done in a series of stages along the horizontal part of the well, starting at the toe of the well and moving back towards the heel. Packers are inserted into the well to isolate the section to be stimulated. The hydraulic fracturing fluid is pumped down at a sufficient pressure to exceed the tensile strength of the rock as described above, creating hydraulic fractures.

At the end of the stimulation, pore pressures will be reduced, leaving the compressive stresses to act on the rocks. If the fractures are left unfilled, the compressive stress will force the hydraulic fractures closed. To prevent this, proppant, which consists either of sieved sand or ceramic beads, is used. Towards the end of a stimulation stage, proppant is added to the fluid, which sweeps it into the hydraulic fractures. The proppant fills the fractures, preventing them from closing once the pressure is reduced.

Each stimulation stage typically takes a few hours. Once a stage is complete, the packers are moved to isolate the next stage, and the process is repeated. A multi-stage lateral well may be stimulated in as many as twenty stages, taking several days to be completed.

Once all of the stages have been completed, the well is depressurized, allowing the fracturing fluid to return up the well, leaving the proppant in the newly created fractures. Within a week of stimulation, between 25- 75% of the injected fluid will have returned to the surface. This "flowback fluid" must be stored on site, and taken to a waste disposal facility to be treated.

As the fluid leaves the fracture system, gas will begin to flow from the shale rock through the fractures and into the well. The wellhead is connected into a gas pipeline system, and the well will then be on production. A successful shale well may then continue to produce gas for over 20 years.

With tremendous opportunity to drill for shale gas and create thousands of well-paid jobs and secure independent energy for the UK; it is time for a shale gas revolution.

To get there, this government will need to focus on five key areas in order to attract investors and ensure that it is affordable and simple to explore and drill for shale gas.

FIVE RECOMMENDATIONS

US style property rights agreement. Part of the reason that there is seemingly less opposition to shale gas exploration by land owners in the US is due to the fact that landowners receive a chunk of the profit when energy companies drill underneath their homes. In contrast, some companies offer a one-off drilling payment of £20,000 to landowners for drilling that takes place 200 meters underground.[48] In the state of Pennsylvania alone, the royalties from fracking passed onto landowners is upwards of $1.2bn.[49]

If in the UK we allowed landowners to benefit financially as much as they do in the US, there would be very little opposition from landowners and NIMBYs would virtually disappear.

Cut red tape for companies who want to drill. Last year, when the Government encouraged investment in the shale gas extraction industry, they announced that they would be cutting taxes on company profits from 62% to 30%. They also issued 176 licenses to explore and drill for gas and said they would be cutting the time taken to grant exploration permits from thirteen weeks to two weeks.

---

[48] DECC *Underground Access Factsheet*
[49] Drost M, 'Landowners poised to reap $1.2bn from Pennsylvania shale gas'

NEW ENERGY, NEW JOBS

In 2014, then-Energy Minister Michael Fallon went to Azerbaijan to speak with their government and gas industry and discuss the progress of the new Southern Corridor gas pipeline that will deliver gas from Azerbaijan direct to Europe.

While diversifying Europe's gas imports away from predominantly Russia, and towards other countries is understandable, it is difficult to fathom why relying on yet another importer of gas is a better alternative to producing gas in the UK. If our gas industry was given the green light, it would allow the UK to become an exporter to other European countries, thus creating not only jobs and security but another economy.

Fallon said he thinks it is important in the context of current events in Ukraine that there is a mix of providers in European energy. However, it is not altogether clear that a country like Azerbaijan, which is surrounded by geopolitical threats, is more secure in the long-term than building up our own energy resources.

Stop investing millions in green technologies and instead invest in training and education for well-paid energy jobs. Instead of enjoying the fruits of a shale gas boom, taxpayers are paying wind farms £30 million to stand idle in bad weather. [50] Meanwhile, the British Geological Survey and the Department of Energy and Climate estimate that there are vast reserves of shale gas all over the country and suggest that just 10% of UK shale gas (130 TCF) would supply Britain's gas needs for about 50 years [51], yet there is very little commercial drilling going on in the UK. If we cut red tape and make it easier and profitable for companies to explore and drill, we are going

---

[50] Webb T, 'Wind farms paid £10,000 a day to sit idle in blustery conditions' *The Times* 4 Mar 2013
[51] Henning G and Johnson C, 'UK has vast shale reserves, geologists say' *Reuters*, 17 Apr 2012

to need skilled workers to fill the technical jobs that shale gas extraction requires. In the US, the Fracking industry supports 1.7 million directly and indirectly.

An IHS study that predicted drilling for shale gas alone would create more than 600,000 jobs by the end of the decade in the United States.[52] If we are to undergo a shale gas revolution in the UK we will need to be prepared to fill skilled job opportunities in the energy sector.

Get out of the energy market – let free markets decide energy pricing. Ed Miliband was a large part of the reason why energy prices in the UK have slightly increased and not decreased, when he announced that, if Labour were in Government, they would freeze energy prices. This is all well and good, but the UK's energy companies must buy their energy at market price every two years.[53] If the price of energy has increased dramatically they would not be able to change their cost. Thus, Government getting involved with trying to set the cost of energy hurts those who are the most vulnerable when it comes to energy costs — the poorest in society.

Counter-act the green lobby and get the facts out about shale gas. The environmental lobby in the EU is one of the most well-funded in Brussels, with the EU giving the green lobby £90 million per year.[54] In essence, environmentalist bureaucrats are giving huge grants to lobby themselves, all on the backs of the taxpayer. Earlier this year, NATO's Secretary General, Abders Fogh Rasmussen, said: "I have met allies who can report that Russia, as part of their sophisticated information and disinformation operations, engaged actively with so-called non-

---

[52] Efstathiou J, 'Fracking will support 1.7 million jobs, study shows' *Bloomberg*, 23 Oct 2012.
[53] 'Energy Bills: UK gas prices hit record low' *Sky News* 31 Oct 2014
[54] Mendick R, 'European Union funding £90m green lobbying con' *The Telegraph*, 21 Dec 2013

governmental organizations — environmental organizations working against shale gas — to maintain European dependence on imported Russian gas." The anti-fracking movement is strong and will only get stronger as Russia's hold on the European energy market becomes essential. The Government needs to push back on factually incorrect information so that citizens can make informed decisions based on fact, not on scare-mongering rhetoric.

GIVING PUBLIC SERVICES A TECH INJECTION

Steven George-Hilley, Director of Technology for Parliament Street, sets out a plan for the digitisation of public services.

After years of bruising economic chaos, at last Britain is finally on the road to a sustainable recovery. Thanks to a dedicated long-term economic plan from David Cameron and George Osborne, the deficit has been cut, welfare has been capped and, since 2010, there are now 1.75m more people in wore.

More people are now earning a regular wage and there are 700,000 fewer workless households, providing dignity and job security that our country so badly needs. However, we may be on the road to recovery now, but history will repeat itself if we ever allow ourselves to overspend again once our economy improves.

The confused wisdom of the left tells us that the only way to improve public services is to pour billions of pounds of taxpayers' money into the Civil Service furnace, but this theory has been proved false time and time again. In the last five years, public services have maintained high standards, despite a reduction in funding and none of the catastrophes predicted have occurred.

So as Britain moves into sustainable economic growth, how can we build a financial surplus to secure our future whilst still protecting and improving public services? The answer is giving our public services a long overdue injection of technology.

One of the main reasons the UK public sector has been slow on technology adoption is the numerous bad headlines associated with previous IT schemes. Everyone knows that when a public sector IT project goes wrong, it goes badly wrong. Take, for example the NHS supercomputer, designed to create a central database of patient records, which crashed out, costing taxpayers an incredible £20billion.

One of the reasons that public sector IT catastrophes are so painful is that, all too often, due to ludicrous clauses in contracts; major providers get to bill the government even if the project is a disaster. The challenge for departments is to reverse the culture of mega-vendors profiting from technical failure, by installing new procurement processes that protect the taxpayer and not the IT giant who caused the mess in the first place.

IT suppliers to the British government need to offer new levels of flexibility, and understand that public services must come first and that their lucrative revenue streams are based on performance-related work. For too long, the complacency around public sector IT projects on both sides has meant that work is delivered late and over budget, and a smarter government of the future must ensure that this approach is confined to the history books.

In this new era of accountability, technology vendors have the opportunity not only to provide value for money to the government and the public; but also the ability to transform public services for the long-term.

The golden rule for government must be that digitisation is the route to successful and cost effective transformation. Delivering a paperless National Health Service (NHS) will ensure that patient records can be accessed anywhere, anytime by medical professionals at the touch of a button. This means doctors and nurses can make diagnoses faster, with the patient's full medical history available to ensure that treatment is correct.

SMART GOVERNMENT: A PARLIAMENT STREET GUIDE

Last year the paper-based tax disc was phased out by the DVLA, and replaced by a digital alternative. In addition to saving a large sum of public money, these processes also made life much easier for motorists, and the DVLA no longer needs to print endless replacements and upgrades, saving paper and enhancing the organisation's green credentials.

Yet these examples in isolation, whilst notable, represent the piecemeal approach to digitisation in public services. The same principles of digitisation should be applied to HMRC, the DWP and many other major departments as well as local councils. Digitisation is a long-term strategy and not a gimmick to be deployed in specific areas alone.

The public sector must also embrace Bring Your Own Device (BYOD) schemes to ensure more members of staff are using tablets and mobile devices to work on the move. The practice involves enabling workers to use their personal devices in the workplace, with access to emails and other services, securely tested and tracked. The explosion of personal devices such as smartphones and tablets means that, very often, members of staff actually own more expensive and impressive gadgets than their employer. With this in mind, it makes economic sense to enable them to use these devices at work, saving the department money and ensuring the workforce is able to work from home and the office.

Anyone sceptical of this approach to mobility in the public sector should examine how this would impact health and social services. Just imagine if carers doing home visits to the elderly could check-in and register any concerns via a tablet computer. Or order extra services or medication at the touch of a button. The use of these devices will transform carer services beyond recognition, and the upfront investment in technology would provide huge savings in the long term.

GIVING PUBLIC SERVICES A TECH INJECTION

In education, for too long digital exclusion has meant that children from poorer families are denied access to the online resources of wealthier pupils. This simply has to change, so schools and local authorities should investigate providing funding for broadband and laptops for families who have neither the means nor understanding of the importance of the connected, online world.

Those who dropped out of school or never had the chance in life to study properly can now log on and digest billions of pages of online information, breaking down social barriers that once blighted our country. The government should work with universities to set up free online courses and webinars for anyone with an internet connection to log-on and view. This will enable lost generations to gain further education that would previously have been beyond their financial means, rebalancing the society and giving others a chance.

At a local government level, online tools should be used to tackle the obscenity that is loneliness and isolation of elderly people. By providing those living alone, with limited means, access to the internet and a dynamic interface of applications for meals, local chatrooms and medical care, our elderly will remain connected and in touch with the services they need and deserve. Online applications should be used to alert charities to those who are left in isolation and ensure that every pensioner in our country spends their final years in a life of dignity and inclusion.

Finally and perhaps most importantly, it is time for the government to embrace online collaboration to deliver a lasting technology transformation which will improve our economy. Cities like London, Manchester and Birmingham are engines of financial growth for Britain, and they need to be better connected to attract global investors, businesses and talented people from around the world.

SMART GOVERNMENT: A PARLIAMENT STREET GUIDE

To achieve this, we need faster broadband, connected vehicles and driverless cars, and better management of traffic to enable the smooth flow of goods and services around our great cities. The city is no longer simply a base for money-making; it is the infrastructure for rapid business growth, job creation and is critical to our country's future. Britain needs more smart cities if it is going to compete on the world stage. To achieve this, the major IT providers need to work with Mayors and city planners to deliver game-changing technology initiatives.

In summary, Britain's public services deserve a technology injection to boost their performance, save money improve lives. For too long our elected officials and civil servants have taken a cautious approach to ambitious IT adoption, and this means that we have fallen behind other major countries in terms of innovation.

The next government needs to embrace technology wholeheartedly and without reservation. It needs to develop policies that are intrinsically linked to IT, enabling interactive services that improve our society and empower economic growth. Above all, it needs to show that bold, ambitious vision that encapsulated the Victorian era and saw our country make huge strides forward.

Britain has an opportunity to lead the world in delivering high-tech public services - failure to do so will see our country fall out of step with a an exciting, brave, new world of bold IT innovation. We have the credentials, the vision and the ambition to deliver this much-needed change and the sooner we get started, the better.

IMMIGRATION – PUBLIC OPINION & POLICY

Mo Metcalf-Fisher, Masters Graduate in Public Opinion and Polling and Director of Strategy at Parliament Street, and James Downes MSc, a PhD student in Comparative European Politics and former market researcher for YouGov, discuss changing the way Britain manages immigration and border control

Immigration is one of the most important issues facing Britain today. Despite some significant changes by the Government to address the issue, it still continues to be of growing concern to vast numbers of the UK electorate. This chapter provides a brief overview of current immigration policy in the United Kingdom. The chapter then outlines the salience of immigration as an issue in public opinion and the influential role that immigration is likely to play in the 2015 British General Election. Policy recommendations on immigration are outlined which the Conservative Party could adopt going forward to the 2015 British General Election and if re-elected to government. Above all else, this chapter finds that the UK's current relationship with the European Union in relation to border control and migration from EU member states, has become untenable. The UK must gain full control over these issues, if the matter is to be sufficiently addressed. It is the job of the Conservative Party to lead the narrative on this very important issue in a sensible and constructive manner, so that it benefits not just the Conservative Party, but the country as a whole.

IMMIGRATION POLICY IN THE UNITED KINGDOM

Before analysing the importance of immigration for both parties and voters in the United Kingdom, it is first necessary to briefly explore immigration policy in the United Kingdom and how it has evolved. Since World War II, migration policy in the United Kingdom has focused primarily on two core areas that comprise limitation and integration. Limitation policy in the United Kingdom has traditionally involved immigration controls alongside a general increase in the number of workers from commonwealth countries in the 1950's and 1960's. The second area involved integration and took the form of anti-discrimination laws. Under the Conservative led government from 1979-1997, migration policy continued on a similar path. However, increased migration in the form of asylum seekers after the fall of the Soviet Union in 1989 led to changes by policy makers and the Conservative government. Various legislation and acts of Parliament sought to reduce asylum seeker and benefit entitlements. This legislation took the form of two major acts which comprised the 1993 Asylum and Immigration Appeals Act alongside the 1996 Immigration and Asylum Act.[55] When New Labour took office in 1997, a shift in migration policy occurred. The New Labour government sought to focus on a policy of "selective openness" towards immigration. On the one hand, a commitment to economic migration was espoused, whilst on the other hand immigration policy was characterised by a tough security and control framework.[56] The reality however, saw immigration increase dramatically during their 13 year rule. Under Labour's watch, net migration to the UK was almost at four million, by 2010.

---

[55] Somerville W, Dhananjayan, S, and Maria, L, *'United Kingdom: A Reluctant Country of Immigration' Migration Policy Institute*, 21 July 2009
[56] Ibid

PUBLIC OPINION: PERCEPTIONS

Immigration as a policy issue has increased significantly since the 2005 British General Election. Traditionally in British General Elections, immigration has not been salient. For example, the 2001 Election was largely dominated by domestic issues such as healthcare, law and order, education, alongside pensions and taxation. The Immigration policy area, alongside Europe was considerably lower amongst public concerns.[57]

Nonetheless, there has been a general shift since the 2005 British General Election. Public opinion polls conducted by the British Election Study and Ipsos MORI in the 2005 British General Election highlighted the importance of immigration as the most important issue facing the country and the 2010 British Election embodied a similar trend.[58] Current YouGov polls put the NHS as the third most important issue on 33%, with both immigration and the economy on 49%.[59] The salience of immigration amongst the public is clear.

SALIENCE OF IMMIGRATION

A number of opinion polls have shown large differences in the public's perceptions of which political party is best able to handle immigration and is most trusted on this issue. Evidently, immigration

---

[57] Cowling D, *'Opinion Polls: Movement on the issues?'* BBC, 3 May 2005
[58] Ipsos MORI, Issues Index: 1997-2006.
[59] Y'The most important issue facing the country
 (Source: YouGov)

has formed a large proportion of UKIP strategy to win support from Labour and the Conservative Party.[60]

UKIP's anti-immigration stance combined with their 'hard' eurosceptic strategy has appeared to have worked electorally in the 2014 European Parliament elections. Furthermore, public opinion data alongside academic research suggests that UKIP are perceived to 'own' the immigration issue and have tapped into this large scale discontent towards mainstream political parties that is currently prevalent in British Politics.[61]

Immigration is complex. Sensible debate has been made difficult by two key agitators: the hard-left, who have for many years, attempted to poison debate on immigration by portraying it as racist and participants of such debate as being responsible for stoking unrest – purely for their own ideological amusement. On the other hand, some extremist groups have hijacked the issue of immigration making association with the debate somewhat ugly at times. Arguably, a form of 'cordon sanitaire' has therefore transpired, with mainstream political parties largely ignoring immigration in public discourse. Inevitably this has no doubt exacerbated not only rising concerns amongst the British public, but enabled single-issue parties such as UKIP to gain political capital as a result. It is therefore imperative that David Cameron and the Conservatives devise a coherent immigration policy which can wrestle control of the immigration issue from UKIP in the run up to the 2015 General Election.

---

[60] Ford R, and Goodwin M, *Revolt on the Right: Explaining Support for the Radical Right in Britain*. Routledge, 2014
[61] Ibid

CHANGING THE WAY BRITAIN DOES IMMIGRATION FOR THE BETTER

As a nation, the UK is currently unable to decide how to fully govern its borders. This is largely a result of European Union policy which leaves the UK to effectively operate two contrasting immigration systems. These two systems are different and understanding these differences is key in understanding the complexity of current immigration policy in the United Kingdom. The first type of immigration comprises non-EU immigration and the second, EU immigration. The first can be seen as more robustly controlled (certainly since the Conservatives took office in 2010), whereas the second, is largely uncontrolled.

The first type of immigration deals with migration from outside of the EU. This is immigration from countries that are not in the EU or European Economic Area (EEA). Since taking office in 2010, the Conservative led government has pledged to reduce immigration to the tens of thousands.[62] With an increasingly sceptical public and an ever more vocal media, the Conservatives have had to approach the issue of immigration in a cautious manner. To a large extent, they have been successful, but there is still a long way to go. A joint report by both the Home Office and James Brokenshire MP, Minister of State for Immigration and Security, published in February 2014 found that figures on net immigration from outside the EU had fallen as low as those seen in 1998, one year after Labour had taken power. The report outlined that "where the Government can control immigration"[63] this had been done successfully through a series of reforms designed to tackle abuses to student, family and employment channels into the

---
[62] The work of the Immigration Directorates (January - June 2014) - Home Affairs Committee
[63] Non EU migration continues to fall, 27 February 2014

UK. These have included the implementation of an annual cap on skilled non-EU migrants by freezing the numbers granted entry to 21,700 up until April 2014. The threshold for minimum skills has also been raised; meaning a higher grasp of the English language is required before taking up a job offer. Skilled migrants are also required to enter the UK with a confirmed job offer in order to prevent long periods of unemployment as was the case before the introduction of the 'Exceptional Talent Route' in 2011. [64] Non-EU student immigration, the largest group within non-EU net migration has also seen reform through the introduction of additional accreditation requirements, higher English language efficiency and restrictions to employment, whilst increasing the amount of accessible money needed for general maintenance during a student's time living in the UK.[65] Despite there being a long way to go in terms of reducing further numbers of non-EU migration, the record and measures implemented thus far, have proven to be very positive.

However, despite the reported decrease in numbers to almost 70,000 migrants since coming to office in 2010, the same report outlined our restricted power in relation to immigration from within the EU, with figures continuing to rise year on year. The level to which EU immigration was increasing was made clear in the same Migration Statistics Quarterly report, issued a year later in November 2014. This report stated that net migration which is the difference between the numbers of people emigrating from the UK compared to the number of people immigrating to the UK had "statistically significantly increased" from 182,000 in 2013 to 260,000 in the year ending June 2014.[66]

---

[64] The Exceptional Talent Route is limited to 1,000 per year
[65] Migration of non- EU nationals from *The Migration Observatory*
[66] 'Migration Statistics Quarterly Report' *Office for National Statistics,* Nov 2014

Although immigration had not reached the highest peak figure of 320,000 in the year ending June 2005 under Labour, immigration had increased significantly from the September 2012 figure of 154,000 according to the Office for National Statistics.[67] Overall, 583,000 people immigrated to the UK in the year ending June 2014, an increase of 81,000 additional people. The report links an increase in EU immigration as the main driving force behind the higher figures. Of these figures, Bulgarian and Romanian citizens (EU2) were up by 11,000 and EU15[68] up to 10,000 respectively. The figures for Romanian and Bulgarian citizens had subsequently reached 32,000 from the previous 12 months.[69] Moreover, as of January 1st 2014, previous restrictions on Romanian and Bulgarian citizens immigrating to the UK were lifted despite widespread public opposition [70] The Government admitted that whilst they were implementing measures to curb the number of EU citizens moving to the UK by means of barriers to benefit access, they were otherwise powerless to prevent the new measures from being introduced.

RECENT DEVELOPMENTS

Cameron's comments in relation to controlling benefits for those coming to the UK from the EU were met with criticism from Brussels. László Andor, the EU's Commissioner for Employment, Social Affairs and Inclusion, slammed what he saw as Cameron's "knee-jerk xenophobia" towards attacking EU migrants as the

---

[67] Ibid
[68] EU15 refer to citizens of Austria, Belgium, Denmark, Finland, France, Germany, Greece, Ireland, Italy, Luxembourg, Netherlands, Portugal, Spain and Sweden with the UK making it fifteen.
[69] 'Migration Statistics Quarterly Report' *Office for National Statistics*, Nov 2014
[70] When asked by YouGov just prior to the lifting of restrictions for Romanian and Bulgarian migrants

cause of the economic crisis. Andor concluded that Cameron was wrong to mislead the public into believing in "so-called benefits tourism".[71] Although the vast majority of EU migrants have taken up work within the UK and contributed to the overall economy, the Conservatives have sought to address the issues surrounding access to benefits by EU migrants. In response to a written question by Conservative MP Andrew Rosindell, the Department for Work & Pensions (DWP) declared that it had spent £1,560,245 on translation services for those applying for Jobseeker's Allowance (JSA) over the period 2011-2014.[72] In a separate answer, the DWP revealed that 23% of those claiming JSA were below Level 1[73] in English literacy.[74] Figures released by the House of Commons Library found that 130,990 of DWP claimants (which includes Job Seekers Allowance) were EU nationals with 67,270 claimants coming from the 2004 EU8 intake.[75] A further break down finds that seven out of the top ten nationalities claiming JSA are from EU member states.[76] With these figures in mind, it is perverse to accuse Cameron of xenophobia. Consequently, it can be argued that it is likely a result of the EU's rigid free movement of people policy, which has prevented the UK from seriously preventing abuses to Britain's welfare system.

In July 2014, David Cameron announced a string of new measures to crack down on abuses of the immigration system. As well as

---

[71] Speaking to the Observer as reported by The Guardian on 30 Mar 2013
[72] Written Question- 20938 asked by Andrew Rosindell MP
[73] As defined by the 'Skills for Life' survey, Level 1 is categorised as the lowest level of "functional literacy"
[74] Written Question- 209739 asked by Andrew Rosindell MP
[75] The EU8 grouping consists of the Czech Republic, Estonia, Hungary, Latvia, Lithuania, Poland, Slovakia and Slovenia.
[76] Statistics on migrants and benefits by McInnes R. last updated 27 November 2014, *House of Commons Library*, p 7

establishing tougher rules for universities and colleges who sponsor international students to study in the UK, and, in a bid to limit bogus student visas, pledged to stop more than 500,000 British jobs from being advertised throughout the EU,[77] Cameron also announced plans to halve the period of time in which European migrants are able to claim benefits. As of November this year, EU job seekers will have to wait three months before being able to claim JSA and other benefits. EU migrants are also only allowed to claim benefits for a maximum of three months, thereby limiting the appeal of coming to the UK purely for its welfare system.[78]

Although these new changes are positive and likely to curb the wrong type of immigration and help to promote jobs for British workers, they still fail to tackle the string of other problems that result from Britain's existing arrangement with the EU; namely Britain's lack of sovereignty over deciding what's best for its own border and immigration policy. The current system means that Britain effectively has uncontrolled EU immigration, with EU citizens also being entitled to automatically reside in Britain without any of the regulations seen by citizens of the Commonwealth and the rest of the world.

Uncontrolled migration carries a number of problems. Britain's population has increased from 59.1 million in 2001 to 63.1 million in just ten years. Official population projections claim that if migration continues at the current trajectory, the UK population will likely reach 70 million by 2027 and possibly higher if annual migration increases. The effects of population growth on essential public services like housing indicate that up to 36% of all new households built within the

---

[77] Dominiczak P, 'David Cameron announces immigration benefits crackdown', *The Daily Telegraph*, 29 July 2014

[78] Gov.uk 'New measures to tighten up the immigration system' 29 July 2014

next twenty years will be built primarily to cope with predicted rises in migration.[79] Furthermore, as David Campbell Bannerman MEP recently pointed out "we are essentially having to build for people who aren't even here yet".[80] Primary school places have also been affected by a surge in population numbers. Research conducted by the Department for Education found that at the current rate, the number of primary school children will rise to 4.751 million by 2017-2018 from 4.060 million in 2012- 2013, despite there only being 4.4 million school places available.[81]

THE CHALLENGES AHEAD IN TERMS OF NEGOTIATION

Arguably the current set up is damaging for the United Kingdom. It is becoming increasingly difficult to manage immigration. As long as Britain is a member of the European Union under the current terms, this current set up is unlikely to change. Therefore, the Conservative Party must be clear about the type of relationship the UK has with the EU. Immigration and the controlling of borders must be put at the forefront of any future discussion. With regards to the prospect of Cameron's plans to renegotiate the UK's position within the EU, Angela Merkel has confirmed that although strongly supporting the UK's continued membership of the European Union, she would not do so at any price.[82] In November 2014, responding to Cameron's changes to benefit access and proposed talks over capping EU migrant numbers, *Der Spiegel* reported that Merkel would consider

---

[79] 'What is the Problem?', *Migration Watch UK*, 10 July 2014
[80] David Campbell Bannerman MEP *Time to Jump: A positive vision of a Britain Out of the EU and in EEA lite*, Bretwalda, 2013
[81] 'What is the Problem?', *Migration Watch UK*, 10 July 2014
[82] 'Merkel warns UK's Cameron over EU immigration' *AlJazeera*, 2 Nov 2014

discussions with Cameron over proposals to reform migrant access to welfare benefits — another crucial concern of the British people, but that this generosity would not extend so far as to debate the viability of the free movement policy.[83] Even if benefits caps are implemented, the issues surrounding the UK's growing population size and the problems that come with it will still not be dealt with.

Alexander Stubb, Finland's Prime Minister and a supposed ally of the Prime Minister, stated that while he wanted to 'help' David Cameron, he was unwilling to consider backing him on reform of the free movement of people. Sweden's left-wing Social Democrat Prime Minister, Stefan Löfven has also recently argued against Cameron's proposals stating that, "it's not so much of an internal market if we develop a market together and then one or two countries say we want to change this."[84] Interestingly, both countries have faced internal backlashes from their own public in response to a perceived lack of leadership in relation to controlling immigration. A poll conducted by Reuters in 2013 found that 43% of Swedish voters outlined immigration as the most important issue[85], whilst support for the anti-immigrant Swedish Democrats party continues to climb.[86] In Finland, similar polling has found up to two thirds of Finns are against further immigration[87], with support for the euro-sceptic and populist right-

---

[83] 'Approaching Brexit? Merkel Fears Britain Crossing a Red Line on Immigration' *Spiegel Online*, 3 Nov 2014
[84] 'Cameron loses support from European allies' *Financial Times* 6 Nov 2014
[85] 'Immigration has to become a political issue' *The Local Sweden*, 9 Dec 2014
[86] 'Swedish anti- immigration party building support before vote' *Reuters*, 16 Dec 2014
[87] 'Poll: Majority of Finns Opposed to More Immigrants' *Yle Uutiset,* May 2010

wing True Finns Party[88] reaching third place in the 2013 European elections.

Looking to the European Commission, the Commission's President Jean-Claude Juncker has said that although he is prepared to listen to David Cameron's demands "in a fair and reasonable manner"[89] and that other EU countries must accept the fact that the UK will not become a member of the Schengen area, he remains committed to strengthening an EU wide immigration policy. Although talks have not taken place and there could be a shift in attitude from the EU and Merkel, all signs are showing that the UK will be unable to fully control its borders prior to a referendum on Britain's continued membership of the EU in 2017.

STRATEGY: APPROACHING THE GENERAL ELECTION

Going into the forthcoming general election, the Conservative Party must aim to take the lead on the rhetoric and policy debate around immigration. It is therefore imperative that the party devises a coherent policy strategy, operating around the assumption that a referendum will take place in 2017.

The Conservative Party must stick to a course of definitive action on addressing immigration. As it stands, UKIP have demonstrated a worrying misunderstanding of Britain's own immigration system and a commitment to benefiting electorally on the public's fears rather than offering a realistic and feasible policy programme. In a recent

---

[88] The Finns Party support an immigration policy decided by the Finnish government not the EU. As of June 2014, The Finns Party have sat with the Conservatives in the European Parliament.
[89] My Priorities, Jean Claude Junker

interview with LBC's Duncan Barkes, UKIP's leader Nigel Farage argued that the UKIP manifesto would have an immigration proposal based on the Australian points based system.[90] Nigel Farage may be surprised to learn that the UK already has a points system in place. Despite being introduced by Labour in 2008 to limit immigration, this system has proven to be inadequate and unstainable as a result of the free movement of EU migrants whose rights surpass UK immigration law that applies to all those outside of the European Economic area. A report by Migration Watch compared the UK points system to that of the frequently commended Australian system and found that as a result of a number of key political and demographic differences, the Australian system was inappropriate for the United Kingdom. Not only does the Australian political establishment promote a policy of population growth, which the UK does not, but it also requires all non-Australian citizens to obtain a valid visa for both entry, work and residency. The UK however, is unable to prevent up to 500 million EU citizens from having free movement both to and from the UK.[91]

Going forward with a feasible policy proposal, the Conservatives must ensure that they are not simply contributing to UKIP's war of words. Rather, the Conservative Party must act like a party of government, as opposed to a party of the fringes.

BRITAIN MUST REGAIN CONTROL OF ITS BORDERS

David Cameron must attempt to renegotiate terms with the EU to cap the number of migrants allowed into the United Kingdom. The UK must push for a system that prevents automatic right of residency and

---

[90] 'Farage Reveals UKIP's Immigration Policy' *LBC*, 7 July 2014
[91] The Points Based System in Australia- Appropriate for the UK, Point 14.2, 5 Dec 2014

access to benefits, whilst being able to implement a stricter visa system to ensure emphasis is placed on sourcing skilled workers. This will therefore mean that the UK will be able to determine who enters the UK to live, work and study. The UK currently operates a new points-based system. However, the points based system has been shown to be inefficient as it does not account for the possibility of 500 million people entering the UK from the EU. As a result, the Conservatives must push for a points based system that serves as a mechanism to source skilled migrant workers, in areas where there are inherent shortages at any given time. It will be the responsibility of future governments to decide what specific skilled worker is needed for Britain at a particular time.

The UK must also be fully aware of not only who is entering the country, but leaving too. Therefore, exit checks must be established to ensure UK Visas and Immigration can accurately record the arrival and departure of migrants. This will also strengthen the UK's national security and must apply to EU migrants too if the policy is to be fully effective.

The issue of border control must be at the forefront of any discussion with the EU, regardless of the early warning signs that efforts may be in vain. David Cameron must make it clear to the British public that he is prepared to consider the UK's withdrawal from the European Union if Britain is unable to establish control and regain sovereignty of its borders. It will be very difficult for the Conservatives to remain committed to EU membership if they are unable to successfully renegotiate on border control. If a Conservative government is unsuccessful in renegotiating border control, yet campaigns to remain a member of a Union that pushes towards a greater EU wide immigration policy, it will signify tremendous weakness. This in turn may have a detrimental effect on electoral prospects for the Conservative Party.

IT'S EITHER CONSERVATIVE OR LABOUR

The Conservatives must continue to make it clear to the electorate that this election will only end up with either Ed Miliband or David Cameron in 10 Downing Street. Given that Labour and Miliband have not pledged to renegotiate with the EU or subsequently carry out an EU referendum in 2017, it is unlikely that they intend to address immigration. Unless renegotiation and a referendum are offered, it is extremely difficult to address immigration seriously. David Cameron has already pledged to reduce immigration to the tens of thousands. Miliband and Labour have offered little in the way of immigration policy. In an infamous speech to the Labour Party conference, Miliband failed to even mention immigration as something Labour would be willing to pursue as policy, gearing up to the election. Similarly, during their time in coalition, the Liberal Democrats have inhibited the Conservatives in their attempts to limit immigration and based on their previous election campaigns, it appears unlikely that they will offer an attractive immigration policy proposal to the electorate prior to the election. The Conservatives must show that *they* are the party with the most sensible immigration policy, whilst making it clear what steps have already been taken under Conservative management since 2010, to address the issue. Voting UKIP will only serve to aid Ed Miliband and Labour.

CHANGE THE RHETORIC

The Conservative Party must seek to turn fear and uncertainty into positivity and optimism, without losing the attention of voters. UKIP have benefitted electorally from speaking on what it argues to be the 'truth' when addressing immigration. It is therefore the job of the Conservative Party to raise the salience of immigration within its own election campaign, but in a manner that spells out a vision of positive change. Therefore, it is right for the UK to have the same power as it has had previously when immigration to the UK was much lower and perceived to be less of a concern to the public. The Conservatives need to be clear with the message that too much, uncontrolled immigration and a subsequent increase in population have a negative effect on the UK's infrastructure. The free movement policy that the EU currently requires the UK to abide by prevents the British government from having full sovereignty over controlling the number of people immigrating to the UK.

Only when the Conservative party demonstrates that it is serious about regaining border control powers from the EU, will it be able to take on UKIP and seek to win over voters who rank immigration as a major a concern and UKIP as a likely voting intention. Once these powers have been restored, the UK will be able to pursue a policy that can fully control for both numbers and the type of skilled workers required, at any given period. This will send out a message that whilst the UK will remain eager for skilled talent from abroad to help the nation advance further, it will not accept migration from those that do not meet the requirements necessary to aid economic prosperity. This approach will arguably help the electoral fortunes of the Conservative Party and help to provide a positive result for Britain's own economic future.

BRITAIN MUST ADVERTISE TO CITIZENS OF THE WORLD, NOT JUST THE EU

What appears most apparent is that in order to satisfy a range of forces namely the media and an ever-growing concerned public, the Government has tightened its grip on non-EU immigration so as to free up for uncontrolled EU immigration. In other words, the UK may be putting itself in a position where it will have to sacrifice the rest of the world for the sake of the EU. Whilst it is much easier for a citizen of Europe to travel cheaply to and from the UK than it is for a citizen of say Canada, India or Australia, the UK must take into account the benefits of recruiting talent from further afield. Providing perspective migrants score highly on the points based system and are able to meet all entry requirements, special attention could be given to those citizens of the world within the Commonwealth of Nations, with whom we share both a language and common heritage. This flexibility in scouting global skilled talent, can only take place when Britain is once again in full control of its borders and immigration has been reduced to a figure that is manageable.

KEEP BRITAIN WORKING

Whilst David Cameron was right to say that the Conservatives would limit the number of job vacancies being promoted around the EU, UK businesses must be able to rely on a sufficient number of British job applicants if they themselves are able to prosper. This can only be done by continuing the campaign to getting more people back into work and off benefits by strengthening welfare reforms, whilst giving young people access to a greater number of skills-based training and apprenticeships. Our youngsters must be given access to skills necessary to excel within the global workplace, so that Britain can continue to compete as a powerful player in the global economy.

A VERY BRITISH CONSTITUTION

While the country celebrates 800 years since the signing of the Magna Carta, we face a growing climate of constitutional uncertainty. Matthew Gass, a solicitor with experience working in Parliament and the US Congress, examines the legal and political battles being fought and how they might be resolved.

What would a perfectly designed constitution look like? Does such a thing exist? There is an almost infinite range of results which can be produced when designing such a system from scratch. It seems unlikely, however, that anyone would design an uncodified constitution with an unelected upper house and head of state, and featuring a highly centralised government operating with little in the way of formal checks and balances.

Many people today are pushing for extensive constitutional reform. They see the British constitution as an antiquated and out of date institution that must be updated for the 21st century if the country is to have smart government. This would be a mistake. Such an overhaul would guarantee a political and legislative quagmire in the short term, as competing proposals are fought over. Furthermore the lack of a clear, consensus-driven alternative means that there would little prospect of an improved system at the end of it.

Instead we should recognise the constitution we have for what it is – something that no one would design, but which works both despite and because of its flaws. Its strength comes both from the traditions and precedents that have been built up around it, while retaining the flexibility to change and adapt over time. It is under this constitution that Britain has achieved smart government in its past and will continue to do so in its future.

A VERY BRITISH CONSTITUTION

THE SYSTEM AS IT STANDS

This year's General Election is set to be the most unpredictable in living memory, and 2015 also marks the 800th anniversary of the signing of the Magna Carta, the cornerstone of the British Constitution. However constitutional issues seem unlikely to play a major role. The economy, immigration and the NHS will loom over all while welfare and housing will be far more important in the minds of the electorate. The constitution is frequently an after-thought to voters with more pressing matters in their day to day lives.

This is not entirely a bad thing. When politicians do talk about the constitution, it is often in the context of a new idea intended somehow to fix what they see as broken. It is comparatively rare to see MPs defend Britain's constitutional principles, and the long history of freedom, justice and the rule of law.

You may think that this is a very old fashioned stance to promote in a forward-thinking publication. However, the constitution of any country provides the blueprint for how it is governed. A functioning constitution is essential for providing the conditions in which we can have smart government. This would not be provided by a radical constitutional overhaul. Recent history has shown this would only create the kind of confusion and uncertainty that would make smart government impossible.

It is certain that centuries of inconsistent evolution that define how the British constitution works have created flaws which can undermine good governance. An obvious example has been the overlap in powers between the regional and Westminster Parliaments, which has led to fierce debates about the 'West Lothian Question' and 'English Votes for English Laws'. These flaws would be best dealt with by the kinds of modest proposals that have allowed us to function for so long without a single written document. The more comprehensive proposals, while offering neater solutions, risk landing us with an untested governing structure that may make sense in the minds of its designers, but would end up as a messy compromise that would prove unworkable in the real world.

THE LAW AND UNINTENDED CONSEQUENCES

With the Magna Carta, the foundation of in Britain's constitutional architecture, turning 800, it would be too much to claim that the constitution is facing the greatest challenges in its history, although the past few years have seen a frenetic pace of constitutional change, much of which has proved to be ill-judged.

The New Labour government championed a programme of constitutional reform following 1997. This included a raft of legislation such as the Freedom of Information Act and the Human Rights Act. Other changes were structural, such as House of Lords reform and the establishment of the Supreme Court. Devolution was accelerated through referenda on regional assemblies in Scotland, Wales and Northern Ireland. Further changes took place, albeit unwritten and informal. The changing role of the Office of the Prime Minister and the Cabinet, increased use of special advisors and a 'sofa cabinet' style of government imposed lasting changes on the informal framework that makes up much of our constitutional settlement.

Despite flirting with ideas such as an elected House of Lords and even a full written constitution, further attempts at constitutional reform stalled during Gordon Brown's premiership. Following 2010 however, they have rarely been off the agenda. This has been in large part due to the untested waters of coalition and the influence in government of the Liberal Democrats, for whom constitutional reform is an enduring mission, and the election of the Scottish National Party in 2011 paving the way for a Scottish referendum on independence.

Most of the changes that have been pushed through were promoted under the guise of transferring power to the people. Whether this has been the actual result is open to serious doubt. However, when offered the chance to enact constitutional reform at the ballot box, with the exception of setting up new national legislatures, people have repeatedly opted against.

A possible reason for this is that while faith in politicians and the way politics is conducted is low, the electorate understands that their dissatisfaction is with the individuals in charge and the political class they feel they represent, not with the system itself. Allowing these same people to radically redesign the system they operate in is unlikely to make things better.

The reaction to this has too often been to seek out a quick fix solution, instead of re-examining their own behaviour. Whoever forms the next government should, instead of constantly seeking far-reaching overhaul, recognise that change through necessity, not whim, is what would make the constitution strong. We do not have a single lone document; we have over 800 years' worth of statute, precedent and convention which have protected liberty and democracy in this country for centuries.

Many constitutional challenges still face us today: civil liberties, the fallout from the Scottish No vote, the relationship between the courts and Parliament and the changing role of the EU to name just a few. These problems won't be solved by today's politicians attempting to dictate their own priorities to future generations. At best they will provide temporary fixes. More likely they will sow the seeds of future problems.

THE CASE FOR AN UNWRITTEN CONSTITUTION

Attempts to define what the constitution is, and what it consists of, are always difficult. Much of it is already written down, but it is impossible to definitively list all the legislation that comprises it. The most commonly recognised starting point is Magna Carta but it includes acts as recent as the Fixed Term Parliaments Act 2011 and the Succession to the Crown Act 2013. There is also much in it that is not written down – conventions and traditions which form over time. An example would be the Salisbury Convention which states that the Lords should not prevent the passage of a bill that was in the governing Party's manifesto. This convention has secured the primacy of the commons without limiting the valuable role the Lords play in reviewing legislation.

Core to this is the concept of a parliamentary sovereignty which holds that the legislature is supreme over the executive and the judicial branches of government. In the UK, unlike the US for example, Acts of Parliament cannot be struck down by the Supreme Court and the executive cannot make primary legislation. Crucially it means that no Parliament can bind its successors.

A written constitution could perhaps more accurately be described as a codified or entrenched constitution. It could do this by effectively dissolving Parliament, and limiting the power of amendment of whatever body succeeded it. It could seek to further limit the decisions of future parliaments by granting full power to the judiciary to review decisions which it felt conflicted with the new constitution.

The doctrine of parliamentary sovereignty has been eroded in recent years, but remains far from redundant. The Human Rights Act 1998, which requires the courts to interpret legislation in line with the

European Convention on Human Rights (ECHR) has often led judges to engage in some creative mental gymnastics in order to interpret laws in line with the ECHR. However they explicitly cannot create new law in order to bring the UK into compliance. That responsibility remains with Parliament.

Furthermore there is nothing to prevent a future Parliament repealing the HRA or any other act. It would be legally and politically messy to say the least, but at the end of the day Parliament giveth and Parliament can still taketh away.

There is nothing wrong with introducing future acts to alter our constitutional settlement. These will be necessary to alter the settlement between the four territories of the UK in the aftermath of the Scottish referendum, and to deal with the other pressing constitutional issues. However we should not neglect other tools for solving these problems where they would do a better job. This would mean allowing new doctrines, traditions and conventions to develop. I will set out later why this represents the best chance to resolves the issue of English Votes for English Laws.

A written, codified, entrenched constitution on the other hand would seek to give away what cannot then be taken back. This would irreparably damage the ability of Parliament to represent the people of the United Kingdom and leave us a poorer democracy for it.

This is why the idea of a full constitutional convention has so much destructive potential. It can safely be said that no one would invent the British Constitution as it currently stands. However this is exactly what is currently being proposed by Labour, who are calling for a full constitutional convention should they win in May. Anyone who finds it difficult to imagine Ed Miliband as a credible future PM should consider the prospect of him as the framer of the British constitution.

There is little reason to think that the current political climate would create a better system. It would be more likely to create crowd-pleasing statements that dilute the fundamental attributes that are necessary for a functioning constitution. However whatever new system were to be put in place would likely prove irreversible and irreparable for at least a generation.

THE 'WEST LOTHIAN QUESTION' AND 'ENGLISH VOTES FOR ENGLISH LAWS'

The most important and divisive constitutional issue in the short term is how the relationship between the different nations of the United Kingdom will change in the wake of the Scottish referendum. Following the vote there has been renewed debate on the various possible solutions to the West Lothian Question. This heightened relevance was inevitable given the various pledges on greater devolution for Scotland that were made in the run-up to the vote and are now in the process of being enacted.

The problem created by the devolution of powers previously exercised by Westminster is that the MPs for these regions are able to vote on matters, such as health and education for Scotland, which do not directly affect the constituencies that they represent. This creates a fundamental democratic deficit.

The proposals to delegate new powers to the Scottish and other regional Parliaments would make this issue even more acute, expanding it further into tax and spending matters. There is no simple solution, and no clear consensus on how to deal with this problem. What is clear from recent history is that any reforms enacted would have far-reaching consequences, and considering the results from the various reforms we have seen enacted over the past few decades it seems safe to assume that many of these will be unforeseen.

A number of potential solutions have now been set out by the Conservatives and Liberal Democrats. Labour has chosen not to set-out specific proposals, instead stating that this would be dealt with through the above mentioned constitutional convention. The Conservative proposals include barring Scottish MPs from any role in English and Welsh bills, allowing English MPs a greater say over the early readings of bills, including tabling amendments, before allowing all MPs to vote on the final stages or giving English MPs a veto over certain legislation at committee stage.

The Lib Dems have proposed establishing a Grand Committee of English MPs, with the right to veto legislation applying only to England. However it is also proposed that this committee would be comprised of representatives based on the share of the vote at the general election not the number of MPs that represent England. This is unfortunate because it has turned what could potentially be the best chance for a satisfactory solution to the English Votes issue into an attempt to hardwire proportional representation (PR) into mainstream politics with no mandate to do so. Whatever the merits of PR may be, there is no justification for using fallout from the Scottish referendum as an opportunity to sneak it in through the back door.

The proposals from the Conservatives are more promising but would benefit from a stronger framework within which to operate. The proposals of the McKay Commission, elaborated on by the Society of Conservative Lawyers on the morning of the referendum result, give a roadmap to that solution.

The reason why a Grand Committee would be the most practical solution is that it is one which answers the question at hand while retaining the flexibility inherent in the UK's unwritten constitution by limiting the amount of constitutional change to that which is absolutely necessary.

The key proposal would be the creation of a Grand Commission of English MPs (EGC) to debate bills which deal with issues only affecting England. Additionally a Grand Committee of English and Welsh MPs would be established for issues which affect the two countries together, such as justice. GCs already exist for Welsh, Scottish and Northern Irish MPs meaning there is constitutional precedent for this settlement. While the size of this new committee, which would physically only be able to sit in the Chamber of the House of Commons, would be a novelty which pales in comparison to the mass overhaul that many other solutions propose.

This body could debate and vote on legislation which only affects England and its passage would be treated as a Legislative Consent Motion (also known as a Sewel motion), a parliamentary device used by the regional parliaments when a matter affecting the region in question requires action by the UK Parliament. The relationship between the EGC and the UK government on bills passed in this way could be set out in a memorandum of understanding, of the sort that exist between the UK government and the devolved regions currently.

This proposed solution has its shortcomings which would primarily occur if the UK government and the majority in the EGC were made up of different parties with incompatible agendas, although similar complications could easily arise out of different parliamentary make ups.

Firstly, the lack of an English executive means the UK government would still have power over the administration of the areas reserved to England, even if it did not have the support of a majority of English

MPs. This would also mean that the EGC only had an effective veto power over any legislation proposed by the government, and would not have the power to propose and enact positive legislation that did not fit with what the government wanted.

Secondly, because this proposal relies on new conventions and informal agreements it would be open to being abused and undermined. For example a government could attempt to justify circumventing the GC by ensuring that all legislation contained aspects affecting the whole of the UK, even if the bulk of the bill pertained only to England. This has been the argument used by the SNP to justify voting on NHS matters, claiming there would still be peripheral consequences to the Scottish health budget.

Neither of these is a problem which I believe could not also be solved through compromise and informal conventions, rather than with a more complex legislation-driven reorganisation.

Draft bills on individual issues could be independently suggested by members of the EGC, or groups within it, in the manner of Private Members' Bills in the Commons. It should also be a convention that the Secretaries of State for departments which cover exclusively English issues should be members of the Grand Committee. The ECG should have the ability to call for a vote of no confidence in this individual should their policies go against the wishes of English MPs.

This would be preferable to creating a separate English Parliament with its own executive. As it would act for the 84% of the UK population residing in England this would amount to an expensive and unnecessary layer of bureaucracy.

Furthermore, an English Parliament would only solve the 'West Lothian Question' to an extent, but unless the devolved powers of each nation were matched up with perfect uniformity, the underlying problem would still remain unsolved. There would still be issues in one nation that could only be addressed by the UK Parliament made up of many members who do not represent it. It is hard to see how this level of uniformity could be achieved, given the level of powers currently being offered to Scotland, without achieving a de facto break-up of the union once tax and spending powers were effectively lost. The Westminster Parliament could be reduced to the level of a glorified Foreign Affairs and Defence committee.

Instead, a cabinet level position of 'Secretary of State for England' should be created to go along with the Secretaries of State for Scotland, Wales and Northern Ireland to manage the relationship between the UK government and the EGC and carry out executive functions as necessary.

As far as the potential for abuse and undermining goes, I have not yet seen a proposal which is not open to abuse in some way and I find it hard to believe one will be suggested that does. This is a problem which does not have a perfect solution. This problem is about how to share power, and sharing takes responsibility, maturity and good faith. This is where the flexibility of the constitution would be an advantage, allowing the new system to evolve and adapt organically over time.

An English Parliament and other suggestions such as multiple regional assemblies throughout England, devolution to existing local authorities or some form of PR have their merits. Each, however, fails to answer the underlying problem of the 'West Lothian Question', while creating new problems that would be impossible to solve painlessly once a new formalised legislative framework was in place.

The advantage of a solution based around an EGC is that it retains the flexibility which is the inherent strength of the UK constitution. Problems will inevitably arise, but these should be dealt with when they have been properly identified and understood. Imposing an overarching but untested solution backed by legislation, when the underlying problem can be addressed within the existing framework, only guarantees future clashes which will only be harder to solve.

THE FUTURE OF DIRECT DEMOCRACY

Given what has been said above about the ramifications of the Scottish referendum it seems worthwhile taking a look at the role of referenda and direct democracy in British politics. This is especially true in the context of the votes in this most recent parliament on AV and a potential future vote on EU membership.

Historically the role has been a limited one. In his 'Speech to the Electors of Bristol' Edmund Burke once said "A representative owes the People not only his industry, but his judgment, and he betrays them if he sacrifices it to their opinion." By and large this has been the convention and a referendum is used as a last resort, only on issues of fundamental constitutional change.

The AV referendum was the first UK wide referendum since the 1975 ballot on membership of the European Union. That referendum certainly fit this description and a further referendum would too, given the major constitutional changes which have taken place under the various treaties since then. Recent votes on devolution to the nations and regions of the UK fit the bill too. It is more questionable whether AV qualified as a fundamental constitutional issue. The question itself was catapulted to the forefront by the Liberal Democrats as part of the Coalition Agreement.

SMART GOVERNMENT: A PARLIAMENT STREET GUIDE

In a climate of mistrust in politics, a referendum can offer a refreshing alterative that has the potential to make policy more reflective of what the public really wants. However this often becomes part of a cynical attempt to relieve politicians of their decision making responsibilities and prevent them from making unpopular but necessary decisions. If overused, this approach only creates a negative feedback loop which deepens mistrust of politicians.

Referenda on wide ranging issues have become a common part of American politics through 'ballot initiatives'. There have been positive cases in their history, where they have allowed the voting public to overrule a state legislature which has failed to act on an issue either through apathy or the influence of powerful interests, as was their initial purpose. However it has been more common in recent years to see the measures used either naively or cynically.

No doubt these issues are often mishandled by representatives too, but the expansion of rule by referendum goes too far in reducing complex and interlinked policies into simple 'yes or no' questions. This approach does not reflect the realities of governing and the unintended consequences can be devastating. For example ballot initiatives on controversial 'wedge issues' such as gay marriage and drug legalisation have been exploited to fire up base voters to influence the outcome of other races. With no guarantee that they would not be used in a similar way, we should be wary of adopting them in this country.

That is not to say there are not clear flaws in the current model that need to be addressed. Historically, a party went to the electorate to enact a specific set of policies laid out in a manifesto, and often resigned to force a new general election when it felt it needed a mandate to change course. This model has not been seen for some time and is unlikely to change in a fast changing world where coalitions and fixed term parliaments have the potential to become the norm.

In the increasingly convoluted business of legislating and governing, people are feeling ever more isolated from the decisions being made about their lives and the people making those decisions. Direct democracy can give them a route through the system that voting for a representative does not provide. The huge turnout for the Scottish referendum shows people will get involved when they feel a decision is of real consequence and they have a say in its outcome. The question is how this spirit can be tapped without undermining the benefits of a representative democracy.

The best steps to resolving this problem, however, do not come from a constitutional overhaul but by making better use of the tools already at our disposal. Much of the responsibility lies within parties themselves. Giving more powers to constituents to pick their own representatives through US-style open primaries and enabling challenges to sitting MPs would go a long way to ensuring that Members are more responsive to the views of their electorate. This should be strengthened by further allowing constituents to recall their MP, not just if they are found guilty of "serious wrongdoing" (sentenced to more than 12 months in jail, or banned from the Commons for more than 21 days) as would be the case under watered down government plans. Having the courage to give party members a real say in policy platforms would encourage flagging membership. Once a party is in government more attention should be paid to ensuring the public is properly consulted and kept informed of the proposals affecting them, starting with an expansion of the Coalition's e-Petitions.

It is common today to say that politics has become broken. There is no agreement on how or when this occurred, but there is consensus that there was a time when it wasn't. At that time, we were still living under this constitution, with its unique ability to change and adapt to new circumstances. Just because politics may be broken, it doesn't mean the constitution is and the conventions that are part of it are. Trying to opportunistically 'fix' what they think is wrong in the name of restoring faith in politics will only drive a further wedge between Westminster and the public.

Burke concluded his address by saying "Your faithful friend, your devoted servant I shall be to the end of my life: a flatterer you do not wish for." In a world of growing connectivity, through easier travel, the internet and social media, we can expect our representatives to be closer and more attentive friends than ever before. If they don't live up to this we can and should demand better. Trying to take them out of the equation altogether though would present a fundamental risk to the British model of democracy which has defended liberty and the rule of law for centuries. As we continue to explore this path we must ensure we don't end up undermining the very thing we are seeking to protect.

THE ROLE OF THE CONSTITUTION

Given how the governance of the country has changed in recent years it is easy to see why some argue that its constitutional framework needs to be updated as well. It is worth considering, though, why the countries that execute fundamental constitutional change do so. Historically it has tended to be following a seismic-level event that entirely changes the context within which that country functions. Examples historically generally include a country achieving independence or concluding a bitter war.

Whatever your answer to my initial questions might be, the result would not be a real working constitution. It could not answer the questions raised by a nation that has just achieved independence, with no home grown governing institutions; one with no defined tradition and experience of democracy, populated by warring factions with a history of atrocities against each other sharing territory.

A VERY BRITISH CONSTITUTION

Nation states are not created in a vacuum, and neither are the constitutions that govern them. Britain has a centuries-old tradition of democracy and the rule of law. It did not always have these however and the real significance of the 800th anniversary of Magna Carta is that it is the 800th anniversary of a tradition of holding authority to account. There are times when it has been far from perfect, but this legacy has served us well in the past and will serve us better into the future as it continues to change and adapt in the way only an unwritten constitution can.

CONSERVATIVES TRUST SCHOOLS

Steve Mastin, Head of History at an academy school in Cambridgeshire, former Conservative PPC in 2010 and Chairman of the Conservative Education Society, outlines how we can re-energise our state education system.

Let me take you back to 1999 when I began my teaching career under a Labour Government. The comedian Les Dawson summed it up well when he said, "I went to the doctor and asked for something for persistent wind. He gave me a kite." Labour gave me dozens of educational kites, having wrongly diagnosed what the problems were in our schools. Underachievement was wilfully covered up by Labour as grade inflation 'proved' that pupils were getting smarter; a broken exams system involved re-sit after re-sit where only the best grade counted; and vituperative denunciations by the unions of any suggestion that not all teachers should be paid the same amount of money with annual pay rises.

The Department of Children, Schools and Families as it was then known, (or Curtains and Soft Furnishings as teachers knew it so we got the letters the right way round), was a hive of activity until the 2010 general election. I lived through initiative after initiative, strategy after strategy, directive after directive emanating from the top floor of the Ministry and the profession suffered from a teachers' version of chronic fatigue syndrome. We just got used to one Stalinist edict after another, honoured more in the breach than in the observance, as teachers like me awaited the next one – another well-meaning kite from people who had no idea how to fix the problems in education. Change is something teachers cope with as it is part of everyday school life, but the changes from a succession of Labour

Education Secretaries were so frequent that nothing was left to settle in. The Department always had to be doing something, appear busy, bring forth grand plans and recommend fresh innovations. All that changed in May 2010.

Michael Gove, when we were in opposition, had worked hard, consulted widely, and listened to the views of a variety of vested interests in the educational world. His solution could be summed up in two verbs: *trust* and *simplify*. Three examples stand out: trust headteachers to run their schools, simplify the exams system to restore trust, and trust headteachers when it comes to performance related pay.

TRUST SCHOOLS

Trust headteachers to make decisions for the good of their school, answerable to the governing body which represents parents. No longer would a well-meaning local authority adviser, 30 miles away in Shire Hall tell schools how they could spend their money for the good of their pupils and, in the process, shave off 20% for the coffers of the Local Education Authority (LEA). Tony Blair's academies programme would be rolled out with any school that wanted to break free of LEA control taking the reins of school leadership and finance. Decisions that headmasters of independent schools made every day of the week would now be available to headteachers and principals in the state sector.

I worked for ten years under an inspirational headteacher whose passion for educational standards and high behavioural expectations of every single pupil, regardless of background or ability, turned my school around. I watched her walk around the college, popping into lessons to encourage staff, proudly giving prospective parents a tour of her school, and walk into an assembly hall full of pupils where they would fall silent. She would have given any top notch public school headmaster a run for his money. In 2010, the Conservatives gave her the freedom to run the school in any way she wanted without having to check with the chap in Shire Hall. Why should only a handful of failing schools be permitted to be free? Now all schools, if the parents and governors were on board, could be free and, unsurprisingly, three quarters of secondary schools are now academies with no sign of turning back. I once asked Gove what would happen if a school made bad decisions and overspent, or standards began to slip; in other words, the school failed and there was no LEA support. He replied, with his usual forthright confidence, that he would let them fail. Schools would learn how to succeed; after all, that's what independent schools do. He was right. What a contrast to Labour who don't trust schools to run their affairs efficiently, don't trust teachers to teach without dozens of government strategies, and ultimately, don't trust parents to do what is best for their children. A civil servant from the Labour years recently remarked to me that many of them were often looking for work to do in the Department, such was the shortage of initiatives that used to be drawn up, discussed, implemented, reviewed, adapted. I like that.

SIMPLIFY THE EXAMS SYSTEM

In Government, we can be proud that we have simplified an overly complicated exams system by making it more rigorous. While Labour kept tinkering with the exams system in their well-meaning but misguided way (dishing out yet another kite), Gove went straight for the root cause of the problem. The exams needed to be rigorous which meant they should come at the end of the course pupils had studied. No longer would pupils be examined in modules after just a term's work, or at the end of Year 10 rather than at the end of their whole GCSE programme of study. Teachers up and down the land could tell stories of pupils who bombed on an exam because they did not revise and their justification for it was that they would re-sit it. I had a very bright girl once tell me she had to re-sit her Maths exam. Surprised by this comment, I asked her why, only to be told her Maths teacher had recommended it since she was one mark from an A*. One mark? Where was the incentive to work hard the first time around, revise and then sit the exam? The exam wasn't a serious one after all and could be done again and again until the pupil got that one extra mark, and the grade she wanted.

Schools could enter pupils as many times as they wanted with the exam boards laughing all the way to the bank. And the biggest losers were our pupils who had to endure this treadmill of modular exams with no end in sight. All this has gone thanks to the Conservatives. Exams are now terminal which means pupils will no longer suffer the drudgery of endless re-sits, schools save money and the public can have faith in the grades awarded. Has Labour agreed with this policy? Of course not. Labour is silent on the subject.

TRUST HEADTEACHERS TO REWARD GOOD TEACHERS

When I began teaching, there was an unwritten, unspoken acknowledgment that some teachers were better than others. Parents knew it, pupils certainly knew it, and teachers in the school knew it. Some teachers clocked in before registration and clocked off when the school bell went at the end of the day. They never ran a club, never worked at lunchtime, marking was infrequent and they enjoyed weeks of paid holidays. Parents dreaded their children getting 'that teacher'. Interestingly, the unions would always protect the pay and job of 'that teacher'. Unions did not care about whether the teacher was any good. In fact, when I heard that one of my teachers in her first year of teaching was bullied by a fellow teacher, I reported it to the headteacher. The unions got involved and, at the time, I was a member of the same union as the bully. The union representative told me I should have dealt with it 'in house' since we were both comrades. The NUT was more concerned with the bully's job than the fact that he had bullied an inspiring young professional.

Performance related pay is something most companies in the private sector are used to. It stands to reason that one colleague who does 'his job' should not be paid as much as the colleague who goes above and beyond. Why should that not apply to teaching? The unions fought tooth and nail to prevent bad teachers being paid less because they knew they would lose control over yet another centralised plank in the statist attitude towards education. LEA control: gone. All teachers paid the same: gone.

Every parent and pupil knows which teachers go above and beyond. I know music teachers who run a music club every lunchtime and then every day after school. P.E. teachers who take pupils to matches at other schools and run trips to outdoor adventure camps in France. Science teachers who run after school revision sessions for those pupils who need additional support in the run up to exams. Drama teachers who run trips to the theatre in London on a school night and get home at midnight ready to teach again the next day. English teachers who sit in their classrooms marking essays until 7 o'clock and then go home to plan lessons for the next day. History teachers who run trips for countless pupils to the First World War Battlefields, or Berlin or Rome to enrich their love of the subject. And all of these things are not part of their job description. It's no wonder some teachers clock off when the bell goes.

I trust my headteacher to pay teachers according to what contribution they make to the school community. To attach a teacher's pay simply to a class' GCSE or A level results would be unfair. After all, a teacher who teaches a bottom set English class is not going to get A grades from the pupils with weak literacy or those for whom English is a second language. Other factors must be taken into account like how much progress a pupil has made. A pupil predicted a G grade who, with an inspirational and dedicated teacher, achieves a D, is impressive. It's not just about the A grades. But the corollary is also true; that a teacher who doesn't mark much, whose lessons are dull and sedentary, who lacks passion, but whose motivated pupils in the top set achieve A* grades is unsurprising. Headteachers know the difference and should be trusted to pay teachers according to the work they do. If that means that bad teachers leave the profession because of lack of pay progression, then the only voices raised in horror will be those of the overpaid union bosses. Not a parent in the land will complain and the pupils will rejoice.

How then can we build on our achievements in Government as we approach the general election? We should trumpet what we have done since Labour cannot refute any of it. But the momentum is with us and I would like to offer three policy suggestions for a Conservative education manifesto that would leave poor Tristram Hunt with little to offer except his manifestly ludicrous Hippocratic Oath for teachers.

REFORM OF OFSTED

Let's roll out the trust of headteachers even further. Schools need to be inspected but teachers do not. If a school's results are very good and parents are satisfied with their child's education then 25 lessons do not need to be observed by Ofsted in their two day inspection. What normally happens when a school receives 'The Phone Call' the day prior to 'The Visitation', is that all the teachers are sent a frightening email calling them to a meeting in the staffroom. No matter how reassuring the headteacher's words are, teachers know that for the next two days their life is on hold. The night before the intense experience of The Visitation, teachers frantically work until two in the morning preparing lessons on the off chance that an inspector might pop into the classroom for 20 minutes and then deliver his verdict that, for many teachers, no matter how outstanding, feels like a justification for their entire existence. I know of many superb teachers who had a bad morning and so they were judged as 'requiring improvement' – which to teachers means they are crap.

What is even worse, the inspector is often not a subject specialist so an English teacher could find the 20 minutes of her lesson graded by a former maths teacher. What does a maths teacher know about how to teach Dickens or Shakespeare to a class of boys with weak literacy? So what ends up happening is the inspector will look for generic skills that he can comment on. Did the teacher tell the pupils the objectives of the lesson? Did she talk for longer than three minutes? Did she differentiate the work for different abilities within the class? Did pupils know what level they were working at? Did the teacher have a plenary at the end of the lesson to review progress? Not an ounce of subject specificity. What in fact has occurred is that Ofsted begins to look at pedagogy without an object. Perversely, Ofsted has achieved what Sir Michael Wilshaw is, in fact, opposed to. Ofsted has implicitly fostered progressivism in the classroom rather than rich subject knowledge in the traditional sense. A history classroom should be alive with narrative, those captivating moments in the story, the tension of the twists and turns in historical events of which pupils possess a deep knowledge. Only then will they be able to analyse, in any sophisticated way, the causes of the Battle of Hastings or the First World War. Being a good story teller is a must for a good history teacher; they go hand in glove. Yet if my lesson is to be observed by a former Science teacher I would probably be marked down for talking too much if I spent time on the narrative and chronological sequence of events. So I learn to play the game for those 20 minutes and include lots of generic progressive skills so I don't let down the school. What a perverse way of teaching.

However, when performance management time comes around in a normal school year, as head of history with 15 years' experience, I observe each member of my department teach history, not teach skills. I have built up over my career an in-depth knowledge of history, the ways in which history can and cannot be assessed and what the history teaching community knows about what 'getting better' at history looks like. No science teacher-turned-inspector could ever do that. The world would not fall apart if Ofsted stopped inspecting lessons. Instead, they should trust the judgment of the school's performance management system unless given reason to doubt it. Inspectors should consider parental surveys to see how satisfied the community is with the governance of the school, the behaviour around the school site to determine how safe children are and observe how pupils interact with each other and with teachers. In addition, they should look very closely at the school's curriculum provision, something that rarely happens at the moment, which leads to my third recommendation.

CURRICULUM ENTITLEMENT

The Historical Association has surveyed history teachers for the past six years. It has built up a detailed picture of provision of history teaching in our schools which is very revealing, and if we take history as one example, is likely to be replicated in other subject areas outside the core subjects of English, maths and science. The survey revealed that the time for history in schools has been cut year on year. In 2011, the Daily Telegraph reported that in many secondary schools, pupils received only two years of history education. This same story could be written just before the general election as the excellent three year Gove curriculum is still not being taught in schools. Some headteachers were scrapping compulsory history in Year 9 to begin the GCSE courses early which meant that if two thirds of pupils (another finding of the HA survey) did not continue the study of history to age 16, then it was not possible for them to study the National Curriculum in the time allotted. Worse news; some schools did not employ history graduates to teach the subject, so your son or daughter would be taught history in Year 7 by a highly competent geography teacher. Or worse still, I know of some schools that have identified pupils at the start of Year 7 who are unlikely to achieve a C grade in their GCSEs so will be removed, yes removed, from studying history at all in order to work on their literacy. Ofsted, by the way, does not comment on this and certainly does not condemn it. It is plainly wrong that some pupils are permitted to be withdrawn from lessons studying their nation's past.

My recommendation is that the Government should mandate that every pupil of whatever background, ethnicity or ability should study our nation's history. This is not only to ensure that all pupils – Christians, Jews, Muslims, boy and girls, rich and poor, whether in Tower Hamlets or Tewksbury – are given the same entitlement, but also to ensure that history's place in the curriculum is secured. I would go further and recommend that history should be compulsory to 16 as it is in every other European country with the exception of Albania. Kenneth Baker's original National Curriculum of 1990 was designed to be taught to 16 but Ken Clarke subsequently bottled the decision and we have lived with the consequences ever since – a five year curriculum squeezed into an impossible one, two or three years. A future Conservative Education Secretary should insist that history, like science (for some bizarre reason), is compulsory for five years. This is the only way we will cover the curriculum to the extent it deserves if you want us to teach everything from Caesar to the Cold War. The alternative is a hotchpotch of practice where some pupils have one hour a week for one year while my pupils enjoy two hours a week over three years. If we can't (or won't) make it compulsory to 16 then Ofsted should rate a school's curriculum as requiring improvement if pupils are not given the minimum entitlement of three years to cover the National Curriculum. This is every child's birth-right and Conservatives should guard it and enforce it.

TEACHER TRAINING

Labour has on its website an anodyne statement about top quality professional development but, as usual, nothing to explain what this means or how to implement it. It also opines that Labour will "ensure all teachers in state schools become qualified.'[92] *Become* qualified? That means work towards it, doesn't it? So how long will this take? And if an excellent Physics teacher with fantastic results but without a PGCE refuses to be 'trained', will Tristram Hunt sack her? I don't think so; Physics teachers are like hen's teeth. Considering most (possibly all?) of his teachers in the independent sector did not go

---

[92] Labour Party Website

through teacher training, does that mean that their first-class degree from Cambridge is worthless? Or the Music teacher who inspires on a daily basis and gives up his time after school to organise concerts will be removed from post because he does not have the right letters after his name? Don't get me wrong, I still believe the best way into the profession involves a strong partnership between university and school like my year-long history PGCE, but it is not the only route into teaching, particularly when we need to recruit and retain the best teachers to teach our children. Another route, Teach First, involves only six weeks training in August before you are dropped into a tough inner-city school in September – is that a qualification, Tristram?

Training teachers is one of the most important ways to ensure children receive the best education they can. A Conservative Government should ensure that those training the finest teachers in the country are identified and helped to expand their approach so it becomes universal. Yet, for example, the National College for Teaching and Leadership (NCTL) cut the numbers of the Cambridge history PGCE, despite it being known to be pro-knowledge and anti-generic skills. This history teacher training partnership is remarkable in the extent to which it has trained history teachers who, as Michael Gove observed, are among the finest in the state sector, some of whom are now headteachers of well-known free schools. So why did the NCTL slash the number of history teachers it is allowed to train? Some PGCE courses are dreadful and should close. Others should be replicated so we continue to send into our schools inspirational and dedicated professionals who are passionate about their subject discipline, rather than woolly-minded practitioners of generic skills and outdated child-centred learning.

Another thing, (which even the teaching unions would support), is a teacher is trained by the state then that teacher should work in a state school. If the taxpayer spends £9,000 for a graduate to go through an excellent PGCE course then that money needs to be recouped through, let's say, a minimum of service of five years in the state sector. If the teacher chooses to work in the independent sector instead of giving those five years, which is his prerogative, then he or his new school should repay the money.

Labour's Tristram Hunt has no such policies, but rather has floated a few ideas to see if they would gain traction. A Hippocratic Oath for teachers was pilloried with mock oaths appearing all over social media about promising to do what the Ministry said, or marking until midnight. And then there was his other gem of licensing teachers every five years, which has been quietly dropped. Tony Blair famously said his three priorities were 'education, education, education' but then his only policy of note was allowing a few failing schools to convert into academies. Poor Tristram Hunt has not a single policy of note, so it is no wonder that the former NUT General Secretary said Labour has no vision for education. The Greens have a clear education policy and it's bonkers, with separate paragraphs about cookery skills and sexual relationships but not one for history. Ukip wants to bring back grammar schools; a clear policy, but fundamentally flawed if you are one of the 80 per cent of pupils who wouldn't get into one. We must trumpet loudly our monumental achievements of which we can be proud and ensure we continue to be bold in our education reforms and aim for the best teachers and best schools in the world.

RECOMMENDATIONS FOR 'PHASE II' OF THE UK'S ECONOMIC RECOVERY

Luke Springthorpe, Director of Policy at Parliament Street, argues that the UK has been steered away from crisis, and the Conservatives must now be bold in leading the second phase of the recovery to make the UK one of the most dynamic, prosperous places in the world.

As the UK approaches the election of 2015 – almost seven years after the calamitous financial crash of 2008, resulting in the deepest post war recession in the UK – several key economic challenges remain. An all-out offensive is required to deliver a balanced and sustainable economy.

The UK economy is still recovering from the damage that was inflicted on it by the last Labour government. The present government has done a commendable job at averting what could have become a full blown economic collapse and/or currency crisis, overcoming significant headwinds (and often popular opinion regarding what was possible) to deliver strong economic growth and falling unemployment. The challenge for the next government will be to build on this success and make the UK a global economic powerhouse that is competitive across a wide range of industries and able to support the creation of high wage job opportunities for the next generation.

There are hurdles to clear in order to achieve this, however. To name but a few of the agenda items that will be in the in-tray of the next government; reducing the deficit in a fair and balanced manner, averting the inflation of a housing bubble, rectifying the UK's current account deficit of trade position, securing a stable and affordable

RECOMMENDATIONS FOR 'PHASE II' OF THE UK'S ECONOMIC RECOVERY

supply of energy and delivering meaningful productivity growth that can pave the way for sustained real wage growth.

It is a daunting and challenging list, but it is pleasing that the Chancellor has been as bold as to admit that these problems remain in his Autumn Statement of 2014 [93] even with an election looming. It is clear, however, that his ambitions to address these problems have at times been hindered by the coalition.

In this chapter, I set out a number of measures that could go some way to solving each of these challenges. None are intended to be a silver bullet, but each will help go some way to securing the next phase of the UK's economic recovery.

The government must adopt a long term approach to the problems the economy still faces. It has so far done an admirable job of steadying the ship after nearing the edge of the precipice in 2008/9 after the financial crisis, but the next government will be defined by its ability to secure the economy for the next generation.

This chapter sets out some solutions for the following issues:

- Cooling the housing market in a manner that does not stunt development
- Fixing the current account deficit by boosting exports
- Reducing the deficit in a fair and balanced manner
- Boosting productivity

---

[93] George Osborne, Autumn Statement, 2014

SMART GOVERNMENT: A PARLIAMENT STREET GUIDE

COOLING THE HOUSING MARKET IN A MANNER THAT DOES NOT STUNT DEVELOPMENT

The biggest risk to the UK recovery is that it becomes unbalanced and action is needed to wean the UK off credit driven growth fuelled by property prices.

The problem for the current Government and present policy makers is how to diffuse the bubble that was inflated during the latter stages of the nineties until the crash of 2008. Although it has at times offered the economy a sugar high and easy tax receipts resulting from stamp duty and associated economic activity, the Bank of England and George Osborne have both admitted their concern at the property market overheating.

As a result of my findings, I believe that there are a number of worrying imbalances in the property market:

- London, the South East and South West take the smallest advances (deposits) as a percentage of the cost of buying a property. In London, borrowing typically covers 62.6% of the purchase against 70.1% in the North East. This suggests a far larger deposit is required in London, which is pricing out younger buyers.
- In London, we see the biggest divide between the earnings of home buyers and median earnings. Although median earnings equate to 46.6% of the average home buyers earnings in the UK as a whole and 54.5% in the North East, median earnings are only 39% of the average earnings of borrowers in London. This suggests that home ownership is moving out of reach for typical Londoners taking home median earnings in the region – £35,069.

RECOMMENDATIONS FOR 'PHASE II' OF THE UK'S ECONOMIC RECOVERY

- A London borrower would be re-paying their mortgage for longer than anyone else in the UK. A worker on the average salary banks lend to would be repaying their mortgage for two years longer than a borrower in the North East or Northern Ireland for example, and a year longer than the average UK buyer.
- Incomes of home buyers becoming more and more stretched in order to take out a mortgage. The Advance/Income multiple – an important determinant of affordability – grew by 33.5% between 1997 and 2008, and has gradually returned to its 2008 peak.
- The pace at which advances have been increased has considerably outpaced the increase in the average earnings of borrowers. This pace was particularly noticeable during the ten years between 1997 and 2007 when the advance increase grew in double digits (in percentage terms) for six of the ten years. This had not been seen before or since.
- A return to normal mortgage rates would entail approximately a 3% increase in charges on mortgages in London. This would leave the average London borrower on a standard 20 year mortgage approximately £600 per month worse off.

This should be of concern to policy makers for a number of reasons. First and foremost, by lending people more as a proportion of their average income, there is an increased risk that the Bank of England becomes a hostage to low interest rates. It should be of concern that whatever the case may be for raising rates in the future, the damaging effect this would have on a housing market so reliant on high levels of debt will skew the decision of policy makers.

Additionally, home ownership is becoming out of reach for the average earner. This is especially the case in London where the earnings of the average buyer is 2.6 times higher than the median earnings for the region. This is not sustainable in the long run.

In order to begin remedying this, the next government should acknowledge that the biggest barrier for first time buyers is fast becoming overall affordability and not just the size of the required deposit, and withdraw government support designed to encourage the take up of 95% Loan to Value mortgages. Although there was a case for 'Help to Buy' as a means of enacting a demand stimulus to the UK economy at a time of fiscal constraints and slow growth in the UK's exports markets, the UK's recovery is now on a firm enough footing that the next government should seek to desist from government intervention in a manner that may distort prices in the property market.

Although ending 'Help to Buy' will assist in withdrawing a form of distortion in the property market, it is important that planning rules are relaxed simultaneously in an effort to boost supply. One benefit of rising prices is that it has been a valuable signal to incentivise construction, but freeing up more land for construction would encourage land presently held by developers to be put to productive use. What's more, as discussed in more detail later on in this chapter, moving business rates away from taxation of property (a productive asset) and on to the value of land (an unproductive asset when left unutilised) would also discourage land suitable for residential construction from remaining undeveloped.

It is, however, important to realise that there are two facets to the issue of housing which require different approaches. Clearly, the problem faced by London is unique to the rest of the country where the main problem is not finding places to build (as it often is in

RECOMMENDATIONS FOR 'PHASE II' OF THE
UK'S ECONOMIC RECOVERY

London), but overcoming the opposition to building on land that is appropriate to build on.

A novel idea to encourage supply increases is the creation of Community Land Trusts, as discussed by Tom Hunt in an earlier chapter, whereby the community retains a degree of control over who occupies the properties. This is a creative way to encourage, rather than force, communities to develop their areas whilst retaining a degree of control over how that development is managed. The localisation of financial benefits resulting from development would also boost incentives for local councils to approve development whilst helping to fund the infrastructure required to accommodate a growing population. Localising receipts of stamp duty would be one effective way of doing this.

In London, the challenge is one of freeing up sufficient land for development. Although government plans to build 50,000 homes on brownfield sites will assist in this, even building on all the available brownfield sites in London would only accommodate 365,000 new homes, while the Department for Communities and Local Governments 'Household projections' forecasts a requirement for 788,000 new homes to be built in the next fifteen years alone.

In the long term, the policy of urban containment via the green belt should be relaxed by selectively liberalising planning constraints against developing green belt land. Given that only 22% of London's green belt is public access land or land that has an environmental designation, this can be done without impairing public access to green spaces.

FIXING THE CURRENT ACCOUNT DEFICIT BY BOOSTING EXPORTS

The UK's current account deficit remains a cause for concern. It is not for lack of effort on the current government's part, but the UK has in a sense been a victim of its own recovery which has resulted in a sharp appreciation of Sterling, especially against the Euro. Whilst services continue to be a healthy boost to the current account, a combination of a protracted spell of decline in the UK's major Eurozone export destinations and increased energy imports following a sharp drop in supply from the North Sea has meant the UK remains in a perilous situation with regards to its current account deficit. The current account deficit now equates to 6% of GDP (as of Q3 in 2014), which has actually worsened throughout 2014. This almost mirrors the budget deficit, which is running at 5.8% of GDP.[94]

George Osborne has himself acknowledged that "we need our businesses to export more, build more, invest more and manufacture more"[95], and has taken measures to boost export potential of businesses. He deserves credit for setting an incredibly bold target to double exports, but it is clear that only radical measures will achieve this growth and cure the UK of its current account deficit.

Although the government has successfully engineered a demand-led recovery domestically through creating an environment of long term confidence, global growth has slowed down. This has seen the UK absorb more imports both from EU and Non-EU trade partners between 2009 and 2013.

---

[94] Heath A, 'It is truly shocking that our already huge budget deficit is still growing', *The Telegraph* 21 Oct 2014
[95] 'Budget 2014: UK firms get tax relief and export boost' *BBC News* 19 Mar 2014

RECOMMENDATIONS FOR 'PHASE II' OF THE UK'S ECONOMIC RECOVERY

The recurring trend has seen a worsening on both sides of the European trade balance equation. Not only have imports from the Eurozone increased, but exports have actually been in decline since 2011, with a 6.6% decline in overall exports to Europe in the two year period alone. Although full 2014 data is not available at the time of writing, it appears this trend has continued. By contrast, non-EU exports have increased by almost 6% over the same period.

As such, it is necessary for the UK to move to a situation whereby its export strategy is focused on areas of growth (ie. the non-EU component). With the Eurozone seemingly unable to solve its currency crisis and potentially heading for a deflationary spiral exacerbated by population decline, it appears the EU's long term growth potential is weak.

In an attempt to boost exports, there are a number of measures that can be employed. These can be achieved by:

Regaining control over our ability to negotiate trade tariffs, and pursuing free trade agreements. This is especially important with regards to the world's largest and fastest growing economies (such as India, China, the US and Brazil) rather than being tied to the shrinking EU single market at the expense of having the flexibility to negotiate our own free trade agreements. This would also allow the UK to diversify its trade, which is currently weighted heavily towards Europe.

It is especially concerning to note that the balance of trade in goods outside of the EU has worsened between October 2013 and 2014 by £500m (from -£3.1bn to -£3.6bn). Remedial action is required to address this, and there are examples of numerous small states that have the nimbleness required to adapt to the rapidly changing balance of economic power by negotiating their own free trade agreements. Placing the long term health of the UK economy in the hands of European Union negotiators seeking agreements that are palatable to all 28 member states is no longer delivering in the interests of the UK.

It is regrettable that EU negotiations on free-trade agreements with the US (TTIP) and China have both encountered considerable obstacles over vested interests from trade bodies of other European countries. There is a clear case to be made by the UK that its situation with regards to addressing its current account deficit is now critical, and that the excessive delays encountered by pan-European negotiation have failed to advance talks at the pace the UK requires for its own export-focused economic policies to have any chance of success. In the instance of TTIP, every year long delays cost the UK approximately £10bn annually, and up to 0.35% of additional GDP growth is lost. What's more, exports would also increase by up to 2.9% if TTIP were in place.[96]

In addition to this, the British Chambers of Commerce have found in a survey of exporters that tariffs and the regulatory environment are the most common barrier for exporters who want to increase their sales in the fast growing 'BRIC' countries.[97] It is unfortunate that the present framework does not allow the UK government to overcome this particular barrier, no matter who is elected.

Nurturing the UK manufacturing supply chain by cultivating business clusters. Over the period from the mid-1990s to 2008, the strength of Sterling and low costs in emerging markets put UK producers at a disadvantage. Over this time, the UK supply chain has become 'hollowed out' to the extent whereby even the manufacturing

---

[96] "Final Project Report', *Centre for Economic Policy Research* Mar 2013
[97] 'Business is Good for Britain' *British Chambers of Commerce*

RECOMMENDATIONS FOR 'PHASE II' OF THE UK'S ECONOMIC RECOVERY

that does exist often relies on importing various components to complete the process. That said, the success of a cluster will ultimately come down to local networks and an ability for local authorities to develop the local infrastructure to accommodate the needs of emerging business needs.

In this regard, local devolution would be an effective way of encouraging councils to foster growth in their areas as well as giving power to the local level where decisions can better be affected. Although business rate retention is a start, there is scope for it to be more ambitious.

In order to assist with this, the business rates structure should be fundamentally reformed. First and foremost, it should be altered away from levying taxation on buildings, which are for many businesses a vital form of capital, and instead be based on the land. This would have the doubly beneficial effect of encouraging land to be immediately put to productive use, whilst avoiding penalising the business for adding to the value of the property they place on the land. That said, exemptions should be made for land intensive industries such as agriculture whereby the land they cultivate will never be built on.

Secondly, just as councils collect the revenues of council tax in order to provide services for their populace; it is equally important that they are able to collect a greater share of the revenues from business rates to properly finance the needs of local businesses. There are a number of good reasons for this: First of all, it would afford local councils greater resources to mould the local infrastructure to adapt quickly to changing business needs. Secondly, the localised incentives to boost growth will be more keenly felt if growth in revenues from business rates contribute to local budgets as well as providing incentives to adopt a 'business friendly' approach to planning considerations.

A mechanism has been provided by the current rate retention policy from the government, which accepts the need for local authorities to be incentivised to boost growth. The problem is that this incentive is made stronger for certain areas than others by having a focus on ensuring 'fairness' in the distribution of rates via its 25% and 50% ceiling on the fraction of additional revenues that can be kept. This is peculiar, given that no such focus on the distribution of revenues exists with council tax. Moreover, there may be very logical reasons for businesses choosing to concentrate on a particular area – for example, the necessity for financial services to concentrate in an international city such as London, or the desire to join a pre-existing cluster.

By choosing to make fairness, rather than localism, a focus of business rates, the government is unintentionally penalising clusters of high business activity that are in fact our most productive areas. It would be more logical for these rates to both be set, collected and retained at a local level whilst using income taxes and VAT as the centralised pots which are available for redistribution as the central government sees fit.

The government should also make small business rate relief permanent in order to continue to encourage fledgling businesses that can in time grow to become exporters and/or an integral part of the supply chain. Given that this has already been extended several times, this would be a symbolic gesture in terms of its impact on government revenues but would give small businesses the confidence that a cost they have grown used to operating without will not return in upcoming years.

RECOMMENDATIONS FOR 'PHASE II' OF THE UK'S ECONOMIC RECOVERY

Paving the way for the UK to import less of its energy. Increasing reliance on imported energy has been a significant drag on the UK current account. It is becoming clear that the supply of oil from the North Sea is in an inexorable decline despite tax cuts on investment, and the UK has been importing an ever growing share of its energy supply for over a decade now, as the figure below illustrates. This trend has worsened despite billions of pounds of subsidies being spent on renewable energy[98] and the government has forecast that imports will account for 70% of the UK's energy consumption by 2025 if the UK does not exploit shale. [99]

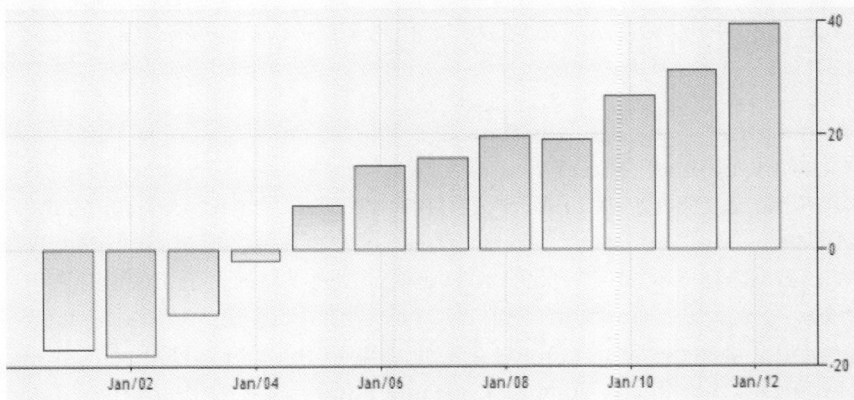

*UK energy imports as a percentage of energy use
(Source: World Bank)*[100]

---

[98] Mason R, 'Britain imports almost half of fossil fuels from abroad', *The Telegraph* 25 July 2013
[99] 'Developing Onshore Shale Gas and Oil' *DECS* Dec 2013
[100] *Trading Economics* Website

REDUCING THE DEFICIT

With the deficit still standing at approximately £100bn, it is necessary for the cuts to be evenly distributed. There are a number of areas where this can be achieved without imposing lopsided cuts that begin to affect the ability for services to be delivered effectively.

In order to achieve this, the government should get spending on the state pension and other retirement benefits under control. In nominal terms, expenditure on the state pension alone is forecast to rise from £87.1bn in the current financial year of 2014/15 to £97.9bn by 2017/18. The total spending on all benefits for pensioners is forecast to rise even more by 2018 from £111.2bn at the end of the current Parliament (2015) to £125.4bn in 2018.

Although working age benefits still exhibit some scope to be reduced, these are falling in real terms. What's more, with expenditure on working age benefits only representing £50bn – around half of the deficit – we are faced with a scenario where even completely withdrawing any entitlement to working age benefit - something no party proposes – would still not erase the deficit. As such, it is essential that pension benefits are placed on the table. That said, it is important that this is done in a fair and equitable way that brings the system under control but does not unfairly disadvantage todays pensioners who have worked hard and paid their taxes.

There are a number of proposals that could bring the spending on pensioners' benefits under control to the extent where a gradual, real term decrease in overall expenditure could be achieved:

An ending of the triple lock. In an environment where inflation is running at 0.5% and the Bank of England's target rate of inflation is only 2%, it is hard to justify the government committing itself to annually increasing the state pension by 2.5% (or inflation, if it is higher). Instead, the increase should be linked to the factors that influence the affordability of pensions. Logical indices that could provide an alternative benchmark would either be annual increases in labour productivity or the annual increase in average earnings.

Index the pension age to life expectancy. In order to ensure that there is not a continually growing disproportionate number of people in receipt of pension benefits who are funded by tax receipts from the working age population, it is important to ensure that the number of people eligible for pensionable benefits is kept relatively constant as a proportion of the population. Indeed, the Chancellor has already alluded to the importance of this.

It would be beneficial and fair to immediately link the retirement age for those currently at the age of 65 to life expectancy. Given that the rise between 2007 and 2012 was approximately two years (from 79.45 years to 81.50 years), this would begin to have a real impact by the end of this Parliament. It is, however, a fair criticism that life expectancy does not rise evenly and that in some cases, health can deteriorate very rapidly after the age of 66. As such, there should be an option for a medical assessment- not entirely dissimilar to that already undertaken for incapacity benefits – to assess whether a person is capable of working beyond the present retirement age.

Curtail the entitlement of those who don't need state support. Whilst introducing means testing is not the answer, there is a rather straightforward way in which individuals could voluntarily 'opt out' of the receipt of all pension age benefits.

In order to create a meaningful incentive to do this, the government could revise down the tax free lifetime limit on pension contributions from the current limit of £1.25 million to a significantly reduced level of £500,000 and £30,000 a year. If, however, an individual wished to 'opt out of' their state funded benefits upon retirement, they could have an increased allowance of £2 million at a rate of £50,000 per year. This would create an effective incentive to save privately for those at the upper end of the spectrum whilst ensuring that state provision is maintained for those that need security in retirement rather than maintaining an expensive universal provision.

Although these measures are bold, it is essential that welfare reform is seen to be fair and equitable across generations. If the axe only falls on working age benefits, there are very real risks that the system not only becomes unmanageable as the retired population continues to grow, but that generational tensions also increase. Although solving the problem is likely to cause a degree of political tension, avoiding the problem is only to defer its resolution.

Scrap or merge government departments. The focus of government should become more streamlined and concentrated on delivery of core services, and the next spending review should also consider which departments can be abolished with their 'core' functions to be reassigned to other departments where they are deemed necessary. For example, the functions of the Ministry for International Development could merge with the Foreign office, Energy and Climate Change should be refined as a Department for Energy which would come under the remit of the Department for Business, whilst the Department for Culture Media and Sport can be fragmented and assigned to different departments. This would help save on overheads and operational costs, but should also come alongside a review of each function that is transferred to another Ministry and whether it is necessary for the state to continue to spend taxpayers money on it.

RECOMMENDATIONS FOR 'PHASE II' OF THE UK'S ECONOMIC RECOVERY

Remove the 'ring-fence' of foreign aid and link to trade. At a time when the budget remains deeply in deficit, it is unjustifiable to have a capped amount on a non-essential service of any description. Although the Department for International Development (DfID) budget is not colossal (£10.5bn), this does amount to almost 10% of the deficit. The next government therefore needs to ascertain whether this is delivering any meaningful return for Britain at a time when our borrowing requirements are so high. What's more, the arbitrary cap of 0.7% of GDP expenditure on overseas aid appears unjustifiable at a time the UK's peers such as the US (0.2% of GDP) and Germany (0.4% of GDP) allocate significantly less of their national product.

Although the UK should continue to support countries that have been hit by famine and natural disasters, aid for this purpose should be assigned on a case by case basis. Where aid is to be spent to assist in development, this should be caveated as part of a wider trade deal that assists in opening up new markets for UK businesses with a view to making development aid as 'cost-neutral' as possible. What's more, we should not lose sight of the fact that the UK is an incredibly generous nation that did in fact donate close to the equivalent of the DfID budget in charitable giving in 2012/13 giving £10.4bn to charities. This makes the UK the sixth most charitable country on the planet.[101] The rate of participation in donating in the UK is also incredibly high, with 76% of people engaging in donating money – the second highest in the world. The government should not seek to 'nationalise' this charitable generosity and should instead adopt a co-ordinated strategy to ensure that voluntary giving continues to be incentivised as much as possible via the tax code and that the work of charities is effectively co-ordinated.

---

[101] Christian Aid Foundation Newsletter Jan 2014

SMART GOVERNMENT: A PARLIAMENT STREET GUIDE

BOOSTING PRODUCTIVITY GROWTH TO PAVE THE WAY FOR AN INCREASE IN REAL WAGES

One weakness of the recovery is that the productivity gap has grown relative to other G7 countries. In the short-medium term, low interest rates has resulted in jobs being retained, but there remain concerns over the productivity of the labour employed in some of these jobs, and their ability to remain productive in an environment either of lower growth or higher interest rates.

Despite the fact the UK has had economic growth that has ranked as the fastest in the G7 group of economies, the impact of this has not manifested itself in a real rise in wages (increases above the rate of inflation) for a prolonged period of time. This has largely been down to sluggish growth in productivity. Politically, this manifested itself in what Labour has termed the 'cost of living crisis.' It was essentially a bet that although unemployment was falling and growth was materialising, it would not result in a rise in real earnings and that job creation would be primarily in low-paid, part time jobs. Unfortunately for the Labour party, both of those hypotheses are now in tatters. The latest earnings figures released by the Office for National Statistics (ONS) revealed an average increase in wages of 1.8% (excluding bonuses) whilst inflation in December ran at a 14 year low of 0.5%. Hence, real incomes are finally rising.

Excellent news though this is, it should not lead to complacency. The fall in inflation that the UK has seen is largely a result of falling gas and electricity prices as well as a continued drop in motor fuel prices. Given that these components of inflation have proved to be erratic and beyond the control of government policy, we should all be wary that inflation may increase if oil begins to return to its medium term average price in excess of $100 a barrel. With a number of major oil producers announcing cuts in production, that will likely take effect at the tail end of 2015, a rise in oil prices from their current lows should not be ruled out.

Ultimately, the only way to sustain real wage growth over the long term is to deliver productivity growth. It is only by ensuring that there is meaningful output growth per hour worked that wage growth will be sustainable for the businesses having to pay the wages – whether that may be above or below inflation. This has been the one laggard indicator, with any meaningful improvement yet to be sustained. Productivity still remains 2% below its level prior to the economic down turn, and around 16% below what is termed the 'pre-crisis trend'.

For some time now, there have been a series of cyclical explanations for why productivity growth has struggled, with many falling down to the structure of the labour market and increased rates of retention. One unique factor of the recession was that many companies held on to workers even in the face of weak demand and lower levels of utilisation. This manifested itself in an increased use of forbearance rather than outright closure of businesses, which saw a high number of firms with declining output hold employment flat - rising from 11% to 20%.

The fact that productivity is now showing signs of picking up suggests that the decline may have been cyclical and that increased demand will see higher rates of labour utilisation. Although another contributory factor has been the decline in business lending, there are signs that this too is set to turn a corner with business lending predicted to increase, with a forecast £66bn boost to business lending forecasted over the next four years.[102]

---

[102] Chan SP, 'Billions more in business lending as corporate risk appetite grows' *The Telegraph* 02 Feb 2015

Additionally, we have the essential structural reforms that have been delivered by the coalition government. This has in part manifested itself in a sharp rise in self-employment following mechanisms that have encouraged small businesses during their start-up phase, such as national insurance exemptions for small businesses. Even as inflation begins to return to more normal levels of 2%, the foundations have been laid for productivity growth that can outpace it and allow business to increase their wages. Education reform aimed at improving standards will also improve the productivity of the next generation over workers.

That is not to say that the UK is completely out of the woods. One element of concern that is yet to be addressed is effectively boosting capital investment. One reason that unemployment has fallen so sharply is owing to the relative decline in the price of labour relative to capital.[103]

Given the important causal relationship between capital available per unit of labour, it should be of concern that there has been a decline in already low rates of capital investment, with the UK having one of the lowest gross fixed capital formations in the developed world. A key determinant of success here will be in boosting the more capital intensive export industry, although it is pleasing to note that the Chancellor has already acknowledged this problem exists as well as passing measures intended to tackle it.[104]

Time will tell if he can succeed in the face of strong headwinds created by anaemic growth from the UK's largest export partner - the Eurozone. In the face of this, George Osborne should make his tax

---

[103] Barnett A et al, 'The UK Productivity Puzzle', *Bank of England Quarterly Bulletin* Q2 2014

[104] Halligan L, 'Budget 2014', *The Telepraph* 19 March 2014

RECOMMENDATIONS FOR 'PHASE II' OF THE UK'S ECONOMIC RECOVERY

allowance on investment permanent (it is currently due to expire at the end of 2015.)[105] As already discussed, shifting business taxation away from productive assets (property) to unproductive asset (land) will also remove the disincentive to increase value in capital assets.

---

[105] 'Budget 2014: UK firms get tax relief and export boost', *BBC News* 19 March 2014

ANY MAN POLITICS

Maeve Clare Ambrosino, Executive Officer at Parliament Street, explains why we need good, smart conservative policies and not populist, easy rhetoric, and questions whether the new breed of political comedians can convince the electorate?

The recent sense of distrust for politicians and for party politics as we know it, which has been growing among certain groups, and the perception that Westminster is out of touch with voters' needs and disconnected to heartland issues, is one which needs to be addressed if the values which we all take for granted are to be safeguarded. As a direct result, there has been an insurgence of populist politics, and all over the country there are small niche parties whose leaders attempt to attract votes with emotive rhetoric and often incendiary manifestos. What these tend to have in common is that their form is greater than their content and there is no attempt at providing solutions. While it may be considered democratic to offer voters the chance to support issues which have direct relevance to them, the result is fragmentary and risks undermining the foundations of our nation. One thing is certain; there has never been a greater need for good, smart politics and good, smart politicians. Indeed, it may well be said, without even a tongue in cheek, that "Now is the time for all good men to come to the aid of the party."

WHAT EXPLAINS THE LACK OF ENGAGEMENT

Perhaps one reason for the lack of engagement with party politics is the lack of in-depth information and a diminishing readership of political journalists. In an age where the public expects to download information for free, the great British press is struggling for survival, and strives to gain readers by churning out celebrity drivel, at the expense of serious political analysis. In addition, the advent of 24-hour news has tended to reduce information to the immediacy of the moment and if an issue is not 'breaking', it is soon forgotten. This widespread dumbing down of the news has arguably changed the way we read newspapers, with many young people admitting that there is little time to dedicate to critical thinking. Indeed, thinking itself may be going out of fashion. In the age of technology where everybody has a voice, there seems to be more desire to speak than to think and internet forums provide everyone with a soap box to do so.

While the advantages in having access to the news 'as it happens' are undeniable, and a platform on which to speak is part of our great British tradition, it could be argued that, as a direct result of these developments, the voting public is becoming disengaged with mainstream politics. Increasingly, it seems, young people are feeling that the decisions taken in Westminster have little relevance to their lives and tend to look for political inspiration on the web, rather than to political journalists. In a society which is becoming increasingly individualistic, voters are focussing on issues which are directly connected with their own interests, whether these are campaigns to save their local park or even to release information on UFOs. Useful and interesting as these campaigns are, they do nothing to resolve broader political issues and the small groups which represent them only serve to fragment the vote.

So far, to cite W.B. Yeats, we have not yet reached the stage of "mere anarchy" being let loose upon the world. However, it is certainly true that the gyre is widening and voters are losing connection with the traditional three party system. In fact, there is an insurgence of small niche parties with made-to-measure policies which nurture the dreams and fears of their target voters, usually without the need to provide solutions. The modus operandi of these parties is to identify a problem, preferably one that resonates with as many people as possible, decry it and promise to resolve it. There is often no attempt to provide details of how they will resolve the issues or to analyse what the long term consequences might be. From the point of view of Conservative thinkers, this type of politics goes strongly against the grain. Conservatism, as defined by the third Marquis of Salisbury consists of "impeding events from happening until the point that they are no longer dangerous."

Interestingly, this phenomenon of anti-politics is not unique to the UK but is widespread throughout the world. In Italy, whose population may be said to have lost faith in the representative actions of their politicians somewhat earlier than most, a movement called Any Man's Front was set up between 1946 and 1949. Its emblem depicted a man being squeezed for money and sweat, a man who was tired of State demands and only asked to be left in peace. The aims of Any Man Front can be described as follows: To fight against communism; to fight against industrial capitalism; to propagate individual economic liberalism; to limit taxation and a general distaste of State intervention and regulation.

The Front provides a template for many other Any Men in other countries; very different from the British idea of the Common Man, protected by Common Law, which encompasses so many Conservative core values. In Common law, the state is placed in an overarching position, with a duty to safeguard the rights of citizens and conserve century-old laws; the anti- political Any Man, is a DIY enthusiast. According to his context, Any Man changes face, political colour and ideology and uses facile rhetoric to gain popular consensus, usually based on fear. Some of the parties which represent him are left-wing in nature and believe that the state should play a strong role to redress problems; others are liberal and aim to limit the powers of the state. Some examples of left-wing parties are Podemos in Spain, Syriza in Greece and Sinn Fèin in Ireland, while a fascinating example of an anti- state, anti-political party is the Danish Progress Party, founded in 1972 by Morgens Glistrup, economist and author of bestselling books on how to avoid paying taxes. One of his more memorable suggestions included cutting defence costs by playing recordings of declarations of military surrender in Russian!

In modern day Britain, Any Man finds expression in UKIP who have a bi-forked agenda: they are anti–immigration and they are anti-European. Any Man, however, is also at home in the multiple autonomous and sometimes pro-independence parties such as the Scottish National Party, Plaid Cymru, Yorkshire First, Yorkshire Independent Party, Cornwall's Mebyon Kernow and The North East Party which render the Political horizon even more fragmented. This desire for autonomy is in direct contrast with the core values of the Conservative party, which is also very much in favour of preserving local heritage but tends to act in the way, described by Roger Scruton; to "Feel locally, Think nationally".

THE EFFECTS OF FRAGMENTATION

While most of these parties are of negligible influence, UKIP, and to an extent, the SNP have succeeded in tapping into the populist fears, regardless of political colour and seriously risk fragmenting the voting population to the detriment of good, smart politics. UKIP's leader, Nigel Farage, by embracing the celebrity culture largely fed by a press which is desperate to compete with internet gossip and win back readership, has carefully cultivated his brand image, using every rhetorical device available. Appearances on high and low brow television programmes, which he uses mainly to ensure we know his face and how to pronounce his name, photo opportunities with pint in hand, the use of down to earth, Any Man's language and decrying of the issues which are perceived by many as reasons to be fearful, have all contributed to the very successful portrayal of a British, or in any case English Any Man. With his self-depreciating,

SMART GOVERNMENT: A PARLIAMENT STREET GUIDE

flawed but affable, smoking, drinking, plain speaking persona, Farage is the archetypal lovable rogue, the flamboyant cavalier, the pint swigging, weaver of homespun politics - The Englishman in the Pub! So efficiently has Farage built his image that his followers seem blind to the paradoxes - that he earns a comfortable salary in the EU parliament, that he is married to an EU national and even that he is not Any Man at all, but is privately educated. The fact that Farage and his party offer no real solutions to the threats faced by the Englishman seems also to be of little consequence. As for immigration, it is interesting that UKIP also wins consensus in areas where immigration is less pronounced - in Essex for example.

And then there is Russell Brand, the stand-up comedian whose re-invented persona has taken him from foul mouthed, self-confessed heroin addicted wild-child to messianic bringer of truth. With this honed and polished image, another cavalier, Brand has become a new type of Any Man and has already begun his steady march along the path first taken by Italian stand-up comedian Beppe Grillo, now leader of the nebulous 5 Star Movement, Brasilian comic Tiririca, Mexican comic Lagrimita and French comic Dieudonné. All of these comics present themselves as anti-political Any Men and believe they are proposing some form of new democracy, a beacon of hope to their respective Any Men voters. Yet they are all anti-political in nature and they hide real dangers to the very foundation of democracy. While Russell Brand is using his thorough knowledge of the art of rhetoric at its darkest, to rally his followers to abandon the voting system, in Italy, Grillo, using his own, can also be said to be subverting democracy, in true double speak fashion, under the banner of greater democracy. Based on followers of his blog, which while it is one of the most followed in the world, its numbers still only represent a small proportion of the people who actually voted for him, Grillo submits proposed policies to his followers before discussing them in Parliament. The mantra is 'The web decides'. This apparently democratic way of deciding policy however, does not take into account the fact that not all of the party's supporters are followers of the blog, or have access to a computer. Blog followers who actually vote, number on average only 20,000, a figure that would be derided as non-representational were it a referendum, are well 'primed' before being asked to decide on a policy and dissidents are not well accepted and are actually expelled. So what is the meaning of this rise in Any Man politics? What are the dangers of this trend of comedians, professional and otherwise, who present themselves as political leaders, sometimes targeting a particular social class or ideology and sometimes presenting themselves as all things to all men?

The answer is that there are many and they are grave. While the idea of being able to cherry-pick political ideas in line with our already established views is attractive, actually basing a party on such limited policies is unrealistic. It is not possible to govern a country based on voters' momentary whims, indeed to try to do so would make Plato's vision of the Ship of Fools a reality. Politics is not a joke; we are not talking about choosing this year's winner of The X-Factor. By weakening a political system which has developed over centuries there is a risk that the very foundations of civilisation, of human rights and of world peace are undermined. The implications are serious and politicians must step up to the mark. Now, more than ever, there is a need for renewed rigour and the political class must pull out all the stops to ensure that the fabric of democracy is not unravelled.

SMART POLITICS AND SMART POLITICIANS

Integrity is vital and it is important that political representatives win back credibility in the eyes of the voters, particularly the disenchanted young. This should not be done superficially. For example, social media may be an excellent way to connect with voters and get a message across, but it is also an excellent way of making clamorous mistakes and should be used with extreme care. When, for example, politicians take to Twitter to ridicule the UKIP voter who drives a white van, they are sinking to the lowest level of political activity. By the same token, pitching Farage against an even more strident Any Man in the Pub, a landlord indeed, who promises to slash the price of beer, may be effective in the short term, in the long term it will further fragment society and a fragmented society is open to becoming a tyranny. As Plato said, "Excess of liberty, whether in states or individuals, seems only to pass into excess of slavery."

Regardless of political leanings, conservative values are at the heart of the British identity and for this reason the Conservative Party has a fundamental role to play in regaining the trust of the electorate as it traverses the 21st century. In his recently published book, *"How to be a Conservative"*, Roger Scruton says that institutions should never be uprooted, but pruned and tended, to allow for healthy growth and development. This is the way forward for our democratic system.[106] If democracy is to survive, it is important that a party's political identity is solid and decisions are taken with a long term view and not simply to obtain a vote in the moment. The Conservative Party has traditionally responded to its voters in a pondered and balanced way and they continue to do so. One illustration of Conservative adaptability is its promise, in light of the British publics' expressed perplexities on the EU and immigration, of a referendum to give every voter a say in our continued membership of the European Union. This exemplifies the Conservative tradition of promoting healthy growth by pruning, even drastically, when required. However, what is certain is that should the referendum result in our leaving the Union, it will not be without an in depth campaign to educate voters on all aspects of the decision and voters will be aware of the short and long term consequences involved.

---

[106] Scruton R, *How to be a Conservative,* London: Bloomsbury, 2014

Therefore, the political system which offers British people freedom and choice is worth fighting for and voters must not be allowed to be seduced by the quick caffeine shot of Any Man politics, purporting to be "modern" and "relevant". They must certainly be discouraged from blindly following a messianic pied piper who tells them that voting is obsolete. The way to do this is through communication and education. Certainly changes must be made when necessary, certainly new technologies and communications are to be embraced. However, it is of the utmost importance that young people are educated across the board in political science and deliberative rhetoric. In the age of the tweet and the quick slogan, superficiality must not take the place of debate. After all, what are the final consequences of Any Man politics? Do we really wish to find ourselves, Any Men, deciding on major issues such as whether or not to go to war, basing our decisions on 140 character tweets, sitting in a pub drinking 99p pints? Surely the British political system is worth more than this?

AFTERWORD

Thank you for reading this, the first book by Parliament Street.

Parliament Street was set up in 2012 to provide young professionals a forum in which they could contribute to the national debate. We do not hold a corporate view although we do adhere to the ideals and values of the Conservative Party, and hope the policy ideas recommended in this book will go on to form part of the Party's policies going forward.

It has been a true pleasure watching the organisation grow, both in size and stature, over the last three years. In that time we have organised a number of policy discussions and held a series of events across the country, including at Conservative Party Conference. We have put in some very interesting Freedom of Information requests and published solid research – the culmination of which is the book you hold in your hand.

If you would like to help Parliament Street grow over the next three years, please do consider getting involved. We are looking for more well-written research contributions and articles; so if you think you are up to the challenge, please get in touch with us on either research@parliamentstreet.org or blog@parliamentstreet.org

Finally, please do sign up to the mailing list on our website, www.parliamentstreet.org, to stay informed about our upcoming events and publications.

Kind Regards,

Patrick Sullivan

CEO – Parliament Street

To Uwe
Great Chapter!
P Sullivan